WHAT YOUR COLLEAGUES ARE SAYING . . .

"*Standout School Leaders: Challenging What It Means to Lead* details the difference between Administrators Good at their Jobs (AGJs) and Standout School Leaders (SSLs). Jones provides a true contrast between the two leadership approaches, acknowledging the risks one must take in order to transition from being good to being great. The text is thought-provoking and reflective, connecting the academic with praxis."

Lela A. Bridges-Webb
Retired Superintendent
Flossmoor, Illinois

"In the crowded market of school leadership literature, this book stands out by offering a distinctive perspective that addresses contemporary challenges with fresh insights. It is poised to significantly enhance administrators' efficacy by offering a comprehensive toolkit of practical strategies and insightful perspectives. Administrators will be able to apply these concepts effectively in their daily work, fostering a more dynamic and impactful leadership style."

Sammie Cervantes
Teacher, Nipomo High School
Pismo Beach, California

"Jones provides a thoughtful exploration of school leadership, emphasizing the importance of aligning daily practices with mission-driven goals. This book offers practical insights and strategies that will resonate with educators striving to make a meaningful impact on their schools and communities."

Josh Chambers
Assistant Superintendent for Human Resources,
Glenbard High School District 87
Glen Ellyn, Illinois

"Jones has captured the essence of effective, dynamic, and unique school leadership based on first-hand experiences, observations, and reflections. This book contains a comprehensive wealth of information that every current and aspiring school administrator can learn and benefit from!"

Dana Salles Trevethan
Superintendent, Turlock Unified School District
Turlock, California

"Jones insightfully depicts the realities of school leaders and shares reflective frustrations and successes of what standout school leadership can look like. He provides hope for what school leadership could become. This is a must-read for school leaders who have faced the realities of our current school systems."

Kristopher Kwiatek
Principal, Bob Hope Elementary School
Armed Forces Pacific

"Standout School Leaders (SSLs) break the mold of the traditional managerial leader. This text highlights those strengths and skills that principals can cultivate to shepherd our next generation of learners and leaders. A great read for the complexities we are navigating."

Jill Gildea
Superintendent, Park City Schools
Park City, Utah

"*Standout School Leaders* is a road map from someone who has done it! Starting my career as a teacher working with Jones, I've been applying these lessons my whole career. It is fantastic to see them in book form. The specificity, nuance, and real-world examples make this book required reading."

Steven Kellner
Director of District Leadership & State Policy,
California Education Partners
Alameda, California

Standout School Leaders

For

Dan Johnson

A true standout school leader

Standout School Leaders

Challenging What It Means to Lead

ALAN C. JONES

CORWIN
A Sage Company

FOR INFORMATION:

Corwin

A SAGE Company

2455 Teller Road

Thousand Oaks, California 91320

(800) 233-9936

www.corwin.com

SAGE Publications Ltd.

1 Oliver's Yard

55 City Road

London EC1Y 1SP

United Kingdom

SAGE Publications India Pvt. Ltd.

Unit No 323-333, Third Floor, F-Block

International Trade Tower Nehru Place

New Delhi 110 019

India

SAGE Publications Asia-Pacific Pte. Ltd.

18 Cross Street #10-10/11/12

China Square Central

Singapore 048423

Vice President and
  Editorial Director: Monica Eckman

Senior Acquisitions Editor: Pam Berkman

Content Development
  Manager: Desirée A. Bartlett

Senior Editorial Assistant: Nyle De Leon

Production Editor: Tori Mirsadjadi

Copy Editor: Shannon Kelly

Typesetter: C&M Digitals (P) Ltd.

Cover Designer: Candice Harman

Marketing Manager: Melissa Duclos

Printed in the United States of America

LCCN 2024051615

This book is printed on acid-free paper.

25 26 27 28 29 10 9 8 7 6 5 4 3 2 1

CONTENTS

ACKNOWLEDGMENTS

The idea for this book originated from a postgame analysis of a recent Super Bowl game. One of the commentators stated that both coaches on the field were standout coaches. He went on to explain that all coaches in the NFL are good at what they do, but there were only three, maybe four, that stood out from the pack. He then elaborated on what made these coaches special. He summed up his list of examples by remarking that the three or four standout coaches "just think very differently about the game and how it is played."

As a career educator who spent over forty years as a teacher, principal, and professor of education, I was fortunate to be mentored by, and then to work side by side with, a group of administrators who thought differently about how schools should be organized and how students should be taught. Among those educators with whom I worked to assimilate mission-driven goals into the offices they supervised and the classrooms in their schools were Marjorie Appel, Steven Arnold, Gail Aronoff, John Carter, Maura Bridges, Joe Crickard, Gerry Jordan, Richard Kamm, Maury Gladstone, John Highland, Paul Junkroski, Tom McCann, Marianne Melvin, George Strecker, and Dick Waterhouse.

This book would not be possible without the expert editing from my assistant, Amy Daly. Not only does Amy dot the *i*'s and cross the *t*'s, she plays the all-important role of questioning ideas and assumptions I make about schooling and leadership.

Finally, I deeply appreciate the editors at Corwin for giving voice to ideas that challenge the fundamental assumptions and principles of institutional schooling. I am particularly grateful to Desiree Bartlett, who patiently guided me through the long and often painful process of transforming many good ideas into a few well-argued ideas.

PUBLISHER'S ACKNOWLEDGMENTS

Corwin gratefully acknowledges the contributions of the following reviewers:

Sammie Cervantes
Teacher, Nipomo High School
Pismo Beach, California

Peter Dillon
Superintendent, Berkshire Hills Regional School District
Stockbridge, Massachusetts

Jill Gildea
Superintendent, Park City Schools
Park City, Utah

Kristopher Kwiatek
Elementary Principal, Bob Hope Elementary School, Armed Forces Pacific
San Antonio, Texas

Lynn Macan
Retired Superintendent
Bluffton, South Carolina

Jacie Maslyk
Instructional Coach and Consultant
Coraopolis, Pennsylvania

Catherine Sosnowski
MAT Adjunct Professor, Central CT State University
New Britain, Connecticut

Dana Salles Trevethan
Superintendent, Turlock Unified School District
Turlock, California

ABOUT THE AUTHOR

 **Dr. Alan C. Jones** is an educational consultant specializing in curriculum, instruction, and instructional leadership. His teaching career includes teaching English at DuSable Upper Grade Center in Chicago, Illinois; social studies at Thornton Township High School in Harvey, Illinois; and school administration at Saint Xavier University in Chicago. He began his administrative career as an activities director at Thornton Township High School, went on to become assistant principal at Bremen Township High School, and then served as principal of Community High School District 94 in West Chicago, Illinois, for seventeen years. Under his leadership, Community High School was recognized as a Blue Ribbon School of Excellence in 1993 and and as a School of Excellence by *Hispanic Magazine* in 1995.

Dr. Jones's publications include articles in educational journals on instructional leadership and school reform, as well as five books: *Students! Do Not Push Your Teacher Down the Stairs on Friday: A Teacher's Notebook* (Quadrangle Books, 1972); *Becoming a Strong Instructional Leader: Saying No to Business as Usual* (Teachers College Press, 2012); *Teaching Matters Most: A School Leader's Guide to Improving Classroom Instruction* (Corwin, 2012); *The First 100 Days in the Main Office: Transforming a School Culture* (Information Age Press, 2018); and *Living Up to Your School Mission Statement: Reforming Schools From the Inside Out* (Rowman & Littlefield, 2021).

INTRODUCTION

*I*n the NFL, all the coaches are very good at what they do. But there are three or four coaches that stand out from the pack—they are unique in how they think about the game and how they organize a team to play the game.

—Super Bowl TV Commentator

The idea for this book originated with a postgame analysis of a recent Super Bowl game. One of the TV commentators stated that both coaches were "standout" coaches. He explained that all coaches in the NFL are good at what they do, but there were only three, or maybe four, that stood out from the pack. He then elaborated on what made these coaches special. He summed up his list of examples by remarking that the three or four that he named "just think very differently about the game and how it is played."

As a career educator who has spent over forty years as a teacher, principal, and professor of education, I have met and worked with many school administrators from all positions in main offices—principals, assistant principals, department chairs—as well as those in central offices—superintendents, assistant superintendents, human resources (HR) directors, business managers, directors of facilities. They are all very good in the managerial roles they perform, but in all my associations with fellow school administrators, I have only met and worked with three or four who stood out from the pack. My interest in writing this book is to identify and analyze the leadership and managerial characteristics that make these administrators stand out. It is my hope that by identifying these traits and giving examples of them here, other educational leaders will be able to incorporate these attributes and actions into their own practice, thus also becoming standout school leaders (SSLs).

CENTRAL THEME

A substantial amount of school reform literature focuses on the critical role that school leadership plays in developing effective schools. The attributes necessary for effective school leadership fall into three leadership models: instructional leadership, business leadership, and new-age leadership. In the most traditional model—instructional leadership—the knowledge and skills associated with curriculum, instruction, and team building are fundamental to success. This model is based on the principle that "how teachers teach" is the foundation of effective schools.

Although these attributes of instructional leadership remain the standard definition of effective school leadership, the last decade of literature on this topic has been populated by the traits of successful chief executive officers (CEOs). This business leadership model is based on the principle that private sector techniques and managerial dispositions should be emulated by administrators in the public sector.

The struggle to achieve the right balance between the educational fundamentals of instructional leadership and the entrepreneurial talents of business leadership has led to a new model of leadership, one that presents techniques for solving the educational-entrepreneurial dilemma. Instead of developing an educational knowledge base or practicing the CEO technique of the day, the new-age leadership model is based on the principle that disciplining the leadership ego is the foundation of effective schools.

Administrators good at their jobs (AGJs) may emulate one model, or a mix of models, but what they all have in common is the efficient implementation of *institutional* functions of schooling: credentialing, accreditation, standardization, regulation, and accounting. While these institutional functions effectively control student behavior and student outcomes, they are poorly suited for developing the diverse talents, abilities, and interests of children and adolescents. AGJs preoccupy themselves with a set of goals that are based on the *what* and *how* of schooling—the managerial means of schooling. SSLs preoccupy themselves with a set of goals based on the *why* of schooling—the valued ends of schooling.

What sets SSLs apart from their main office colleagues is how they think about and respond to school structures that are fundamentally opposed to mission-driven goals and values. AGJs view the dilemma of institutional schooling as an *either/or* proposition, where institutional means take precedence over educational ends. SSLs view the dilemma of institutional schooling as a *both/and* proposition, where institutional means work together with educational ends to create mission-driven learning environments. Each chapter in this book describes the organizational strategies and habits of thought that SSLs employ to maintain the smooth running of schools that fit a community's expectation of what schooling should look like, yet at the same time foster innovative teaching environments that fit a student body's expectation for how schooling should *feel*.

> *SSLs view the dilemma of institutional schooling as a both/and proposition, where institutional means work together with educational ends to create mission-driven learning environments.*

WHAT IS A MISSION-DRIVEN SCHOOL?

A fundamental principle in school organizations is the belief in and adherence to the educational goals and values written in school mission statements. School mission statements include one or more of the mission-driven goals and values listed in Figure I.1. All school administrators publicly promote the educational goals and values written in their school mission statements, but they rarely admit to the institutional values that too often drive the operations of the schools they lead. SSLs take on the challenge of creating schools organized around the mission rather than falling back on traditional, institutional practices in their day-to-day administration. Each chapter in this book describes the contrasts between how AGJs and SSLs approach the underlying struggle between institutional and educational goals and values, allowing AGJs to move further along the continuum toward becoming SSLs.

FIGURE I.1 AIMING FOR MISSION-DRIVEN SCHOOLS

INSTITUTIONAL-DRIVEN SCHOOLS		MISSION-DRIVEN SCHOOLS	
VALUE/ATTRIBUTE	GOAL	VALUE/ATTRIBUTE	GOAL
School centered	To follow directions	Child centered	To develop agency
Uniformity	To accurately classify	Diversity	To develop a sense of belongingness
Preparation	To develop skills	Life-long learning	To develop an interest
Replicative thinking	To recite knowledge	Critical thinking	To develop knowledge

AUDIENCE

In the last decade, state governmental bodies, professional educational organizations, think-tanks of all political persuasions, and a number of notable CEOs and successful entrepreneurs have called for the radical transformation of the way we "do schooling" in this nation. Proponents of these reform efforts have all reached the same conclusion: Real change in how schools are organized and how teachers teach is wholly dependent on the leadership abilities of the people who sit in main offices.

While there is no disagreement about the critical role leadership plays in any transformational process, the institutional realities of schooling established by governmental and private bodies—mandates, accreditation, certification, safety, and accountability—are in direct opposition to the innovative thinking, dispositions, and practices that these reform proponents promote. This book is aimed at administrators who observe and experience the gap between managing their schools well but falling short of mission-driven goals and values listed in their school mission statements. *Standout School Leaders: Challenging What It Means to Lead* offers guidance on how school administrators and potential school leaders can challenge the institutional realities of the schools they lead and develop the kinds of learning experiences described in their school mission statements.

WHAT MAKES THIS BOOK DISTINCTIVE

This book is not a how-to guide to become an SSL or a list of research findings on effective school leadership. The book begins with the acknowledgement that school administrators have in their careers mastered the knowledge, skills, and dispositions to manage their schools well—they are administrators good at their jobs. A school that is *doing things well*, however, isn't necessarily *doing the right things*. Each chapter in this book provides answers to questions that school administrators wrestle with and helps them develop tools and strategies to do the *right things*—closing that gap between the *is* and *ought to be* of schooling. Applying these strategies to their own practice will help administrators focus less on smooth management (the *what* and *how*) and more

on their mission (the *why*), moving them toward becoming SSLs. To help leaders in that endeavor, this book provides practical features and resources.

FEATURES AND BENEFITS

- **Chapter openers:** Each chapter begins with a description of a fundamental administrative function that is interpreted and performed in differing ways by SSLs and AGJs.

- **Conversation excerpts:** The opening of each chapter brings the reader into school office conversations where SSLs and AGJs present their opposing philosophies on the *what*, *why*, and *how* of schooling.

- **Vignettes:** Throughout the chapters the reader is presented with managerial and leadership scenarios that school administrators face every day. Each situation calls upon an administrator to make an institutional or mission-driven response. As the reader progresses from chapter to chapter, a pattern of behaviors emerges showing the differing managerial and leadership responses of SSLs and AGJs.

- **Figures and tools:** Throughout the book readers will find several tables and figures that summarize the key managerial and leadership concepts presented in each chapter. These figures serve as practical tools that school leaders can reference when applying the managerial and leadership practices developed in each chapter.

- **SSL tips:** Each chapter ends with an insight into how SSLs think differently about the goals and practices of schooling.

- **Reflective questions:** These questions help readers reflect on the content of the chapter and invite the reader to apply the insights of the chapter to their own practices and school sites.

- **End-of-chapter resources:** Each chapter provides the reader with resources that elaborate on the managerial and leadership concepts developed in the chapter.

All of these features provide readers with abbreviated versions of the managerial and leadership concepts developed in each chapter. They serve as practical and applicable tools that school leaders can immediately apply to improve their practice.

CHAPTER 1

....

BEING GOOD
AT THE JOB

In this chapter I discuss how simply ensuring smooth school operations is not enough to stand out. The conversations that follow illustrate seven essential managerial functions that all AGJs master and perform on a daily basis—necessary to demonstrate managerial competence, but insufficient for becoming an SSL.

Principal to Class of 2025 (Communication)	"Welcome to our first open house. Mr. Davies will provide you with the schedule we will follow tonight. Before we proceed with tonight's activities, I want to take a few minutes to discuss our staff's commitment to excellence. In my last newsletter, I described several initiatives we have undertaken to raise the academic bar in our school. Among those that we believe show the most promise is the adoption of our online student gradebook program.
	"Additionally, in our classrooms tonight you will hear references to our Central High Scholar program. This program is designed to provide all students with the technologies and tutorial services they will need to meet the criteria for becoming a Central High scholar. I've asked several Central High scholars to make a brief presentation during our break about the programs that most helped them achieve academic excellence."
Board Member to Principal (Organization)	"Dr. Lorenzo, I would like to commend you on providing all our students with full schedules on the first day of school. As you know, in the past we have had too many students in the counselor's office on the first day of school waiting to be scheduled for classes they registered for."
Principal to Parent (Outreach)	"Hope to see you at our spring booster barbecue event. Great ribs and, as always, our booster chairperson, Mary, will put together the best silent raffle in the conference."

(Continued)

(Continued)

Union Representative to Principal (Mediation)	"Dr. Lorenzo, would you consider moving Ms. Jane Ferguson to the media center? I recognize the problems she is having in the classroom, but she has always been a loyal, dependable, and tireless educator."
Parent to Principal (Negotiation)	"Dr. Lorenzo, would it be possible to use the gym one night a week for our community soccer league? Our league can't afford to pay the fees for park district facilities. I know some of our varsity teams have these facilities scheduled year-round, but our league gives our Latino youth an opportunity to participate in a worthwhile after-school activity."
Principal's Post to the Faculty Page on Facebook (Cheerleading)	🎉 WELCOME BACK, PANTHERS! 🎉 The halls of Central High are buzzing with excitement as we kick off another fantastic year! Whether you're a returning student or one of our new Panthers, we're thrilled to have you as part of our incredible community. This year, we're setting the stage for success with our theme: **"Leading with Panther pride!"** Let's bring our energy, enthusiasm, and commitment to make this year our best one yet. Together, we'll inspire, challenge, and achieve greatness. Here's to a year filled with Panther pride, growth, and endless possibilities! 🐾 Go Panthers! 🐾 Dr. Lorenzo Principal
Superintendent to Board of Education (Personalization)	"I'd like to congratulate Principal Lorenzo on acquiring and implementing our new finance management software package. With this program in place, we now have a process for cost-effective decision-making."

BEING VERY GOOD AT YOUR JOB

The introduction to this book presented the idea that while there are many football coaches—and school administrators—who are good at the job, there are very few who stand out. Here I summarize the knowledge and skills that all school administrators must possess and enact on a daily basis to be perceived by the school community as doing the job well. Mastering these skills is no small feat; being an AGJ is a great achievement. However, while these skills are necessary for demonstrating managerial proficiency, they are not enough to become an SSL. In fact, if they are not moderated, they can become enemies to standout school leadership.

Communication

AGJs are effective communicators. They use a variety of methods to communicate their message to the stakeholders in the school community. They assure parents, faculty, and students that their school has high standards of excellence. They share ideas and plans and invite these stakeholders to be participants. They discuss the structures that are in place to ensure that the school embraces diversity and provides a safe environment for all. To become an SSL, however, administrators must do more than this. Aspiring SSLs author and communicate the particulars of these qualities of schooling. These particulars might include innovative instructional programs, inventive measures to address problematic programs, or overhauls of poorly functioning building systems. Taking these extra steps will help AGJs stand out.

Organization

AGJs are effective implementers. They pay close attention to the efficient and effective operations of the systems that parents and the district depend upon. Buses arrive on time, student schedules are correct, school events are executed well, the school facility is clean and orderly, budgets are balanced, reports are filed on time, and all state rules and regulations are followed. Each of these schoolwide functions is the result of well-established managerial tasks designed to comply with directives arriving in a main office inbox. To become an SSL, administrators must do more than ensure the smooth running of these logistical processes. Aspiring SSLs redesign organizational systems that are serving as obstacles to achieving mission-driven goals or entangling students and parents in bureaucratic mazes. SSLs are careful not to allow the institutional values of efficiency and order to overshadow the educational values of developing the individual abilities, talents, and interests of diverse student populations. SSLs create engaging educational experiences. Taking this extra step will help AGJs stand out.

Outreach

AGJs are effective at public relations. Main offices have formal channels of communication such as newsletters, webpages, and scheduled community events to inform the public of the goals, programs, and activities most valued by parents. Most administrators, however, choose informal channels for communicating these goals, programs, and activities. The favored informal channel is through working public gatherings. Circulating during various social functions, principals greet parents with a narrative that goes something like this:

> John, so glad to see you! I know your work schedule makes it difficult to attend these games. Your son Dan had a great season! His last-minute shot last week put us into the regionals. I see he's

active in our Model United Nations program. We started that program last year to balance out our offerings in the humanities department. Hope to see you at the spring booster barbecue event. Great ribs and, as always, our booster chairperson, Mary, has put together the best silent raffle in the conference.

At the end of these parent gatherings, AGJs have achieved the goal of putting a human face to what often appears to be a faceless bureaucracy. To become an SSL, administrators must do more than this. Aspiring SSLs use these informal gatherings as opportunities to *listen* for "sticking points" in their school's organizational structure or instructional program that are serving as barriers to developing the individualities of students or that marginalize the participation of differing demographic groups in the community (see vignette titled "Enhancing Engagement With Dual Open Houses"). They move those sticking points to the top of their personal calendars and to the top of team meeting agendas to create educational environments conducive to developing the individualities of diverse student populations. Taking these extra steps will help AGJs stand out.

> *Aspiring SSLs use these informal gatherings as opportunities to* listen *for "sticking points" in their school's organizational structure or instructional program that are serving as barriers to developing the individualities of students or that marginalize the participation of differing demographic groups in the community.*

ENHANCING ENGAGEMENT WITH DUAL OPEN HOUSES
Maria Dominquez (community outreach director) and Theodore Wallace (principal)

Ms. Dominguez: Dr. Wallace, would you be open to setting up a separate open house for our Spanish-speaking families?

Principal Wallace: What's the problem with our current open house?

Ms. Dominguez: The format works very well for most of our school community, but not so well for our Spanish-speaking families. That's why their attendance at our open house nights is low.

Principal Wallace: What would you suggest?

Ms. Dominguez: Our community is much more comfortable in a more informal setting.

Principal Wallace: Informal setting?

Ms. Dominguez:	Well, some Hispanic parents are uncomfortable with the formality of the night: walking to classrooms every ten minutes, following a bell schedule, and formal presentations by teachers in a language they often don't understand well. It just doesn't work for our community."
Principal Wallace:	Well, what would work?
Ms. Dominguez:	After brainstorming at the Bilingual Department meeting, we identified an open house format that prioritizes effective communication with our parents. We could hold the open house in the media center. There's enough room to accommodate a seating area and open areas where parents have an opportunity to visit with neighbors, friends, and relatives. We would set up tables by the computer room for a potluck dinner before the presentation. Bilingual program teachers Julio Garcia and Margaret Johnson have volunteered to make a presentation on the goals of the program and recommendations on how parents could support their children's schooling. Several teachers from the regular academic program, along with teachers in the Bilingual Department, would sit at tables near the TV studio to answer questions about their courses and, if asked, report to parents on their children's progress. Several faculty members and students from our Spanish classes have volunteered as translators. Oh, one more thing, Dr. Wallace: Mrs. Ashanti from the Home Economics Department said students from her childcare course would provide a babysitting service for the night."
Principal Wallace:	Ms. Dominguez, you've certainly done your homework on this. While I see the need for such a night and applaud you for all the work you put into planning it, let me tell you about the obstacles that I'll face if I try to do this. First, I have at least three board members who feel that we shouldn't even have a bilingual program in our school. They firmly believe that learning a second language is best achieved by full immersion in the language of the host country. Secondly, I know I will have faculty members who will question a program that appears to support a 'separate but equal status' for our Hispanic students. Just recently, the mayor made several comments in our local press questioning signs and advertisements for local merchants that are in Spanish.
Ms. Dominguez:	I know you are a strong supporter of our program. I don't want to put you in a bad position with the board or faculty, but I know you're concerned about the lack of attendance of Hispanic parents at school events. I was just looking for ways to bring my community back into the school. Maybe we can work at softening up the critics this year and plan for next year's open house.

(Continued)

(Continued)

Principal Wallace:	No, Ms. Dominguez, we'll do a bilingual open house this year. I'll call it a pilot program. Let me get the ball rolling with the space and furniture arrangements. You seem to have done the heavy lifting with the program. I'll get a letter to parents in your community about the changes in the program.
Ms. Dominguez:	No need for the letter. I'll spread the word to the families and the teachers in the Bilingual Department can talk to their students about the program change.
Principal Wallace:	Ms. Dominguez, thanks again for all the thought and planning that went into reformatting our open house to increase participation by our Hispanic families.
Ms. Dominguez:	Dr. Wallace, I can't believe this happening! Oh, one more thing, do you think we could have mariachi band perform at the end of the evening? We have several really good bands in our community.
Principal Wallace:	Let's think about the band for next year.

Mediation

AGJs are effective peacekeepers. The entire professional infrastructure of public schooling in this country is grounded in the beliefs, values, and practices of a bureaucratic model of schooling that is perfectly suited to satisfy institutional goals: standardization, compliance, and documentation. However, these functions are not well suited to achieving educational goals: interests, agency, and critical thinking.

The gap between educational goals and institutional realities generates daily conflicts between organizational structures designed to routinize and instructional programs designed to honor the diverse interests, talents, and lifestyles of their student bodies. When these conflicts disrupt organizational and instructional routines, AGJs employ a variety of work-around strategies that soften the rough edges of bureaucratic schooling, such as offering extra time, extra credit, or extra help. To become an SSL, administrators must do more than this—they must openly acknowledge the existence of these rough edges and enact specific administrative measures to smooth them. Aspiring SSLs reconcile institutional goals with practices that enhance the individual interests, talents, and abilities of staff and students. SSLs are careful not

> *SSLs are careful not to allow the softening of bureaucratic rough edges to interfere with maintaining a safe and orderly school environment.*

to allow the softening of bureaucratic rough edges to interfere with maintaining a safe and orderly school environment. Taking these extra steps will help AGJs stand out.

Negotiation

AGJs are effective diplomats. Every school district is packed with special interest groups competing for limited resources. In addition to the special interest groups of the school community, an array of local and state governmental agencies, community groups, professional organizations, and private vendors also influence different segments of the school organization.

AGJs keep all these groups invested in the goals and operations of the school by manipulating different resource variables—time, space, personnel, materials, and fundraising activities—to create an image of perceived fairness among all interest groups. To become an SSL, administrators must do more than just engage in this political gamesmanship. Aspiring SSLs must make a distinction between the equal distribution of resources and the distribution of resources based on the different circumstances of the groups they serve. SSLs aim to distribute resources in ways that provide different groups the opportunities to reach equal outcomes. SSLs are careful not to allow their redefinition of fairness to be perceived by the school community as favoring certain groups or activities.

Motivators

AGJs are effective motivators. Teachers do not work well in environments that are externally controlled and competitive. AGJs translate teacher distaste for being supervised and rated into superficial dispositions that will make them a "good boss" in the eyes of their faculty (see Resource 1.1 for examples of these superficial dispositions). To become an SSL, administrators must do more than cater to teachers' need for approval. Aspiring SSLs are sensitive to the social, emotional, and intellectual harm that poor teaching can inflict on children and adolescents. Establishing performance standards and helping staff continually improve to meet those standards will make AGJs stand out.

Personalization

AGJs are effective optimizers. They recognize and harness their unique personal and professional interests—what I term *bents* (see Resource 1.2). A particular administrator's bent may come in handy for resolving a schoolwide problem that established managerial tools have failed to fix. To become an SSL, however, administrators must do more than focus on their own interests. Aspiring SSLs must consider both their own bents and the bents of their colleagues and optimize them to directly advance the educational mission of schooling. Taking this extra step will help AGJs stand out.

SSL TIP

Why Being Good at Your Job Is Not Good Enough

There is no question that these managerial tasks and functions are essential for *doing things right.* Like AGJs, SSLs accept the necessity of performing well the managerial tasks and functions summarized in this chapter. SSLs, however, stand out from their colleagues by asking, "Are we doing the right things?" Listed here are the types of value-added questions that an SSL would ask regarding the managerial functions they perform each day:

- Will raising the academic bar in the school create learning environments that enhance the diverse interests, talents, and abilities of children and adolescents?

- Will well-choreographed social events signify a caring and respectful learning environment?

- Will attendance at social gatherings advance the educational goals of the school?

- Will the adoption of learning standards compensate for monotonous teaching regimes?

- Will allocation of resources represent equal opportunities for all community groups?

- Will high staff morale result in high staff performance?

- Will the effective implementation of programs symbolize a quality educational program?

These are the responses that SSLs might formulate for these valued-added questions:

- Moving a struggling teacher into a nonteaching position would maintain high teacher morale at the expense of compromising established classroom performance standards.

- The focus on *compliance* with accountability mandates would come at the expense of fulfilling the *substance* of the mandates.

- The focus on raising student test scores would come at the expense of creating learning experiences that would enhance the diverse talents, abilities, and interest of children and adolescents.

These answers would identify which managerial functions are worth pursuing and which should be modified or abandoned. The remaining chapters in this book will describe how SSLs create organizational and instructional systems that *do the right things well.*

1. As you think about the content of the certification programs you completed, which bents (see Resource 1.2) were emphasized and which bents received little or no attention? Why do you believe these program priorities were established?

2. In reviewing your past performance evaluations, what administrative functions received little or no attention? Why do you believe these administrative functions go unnoticed or receive a cursory comment?

3. Recent surveys of job satisfaction of principals found that a majority expressed frustration with their inability to spend more time on supervising instruction. They cited the following reasons for their inattention to classroom supervision: putting out fires, complying with district and governmental directives and mandates, and managing operating building systems. If you agree with these survey results, what strategies would you adopt to spend more time on the central mission of schooling—to educate?

4. As you think about the various bents of the school leaders in your building, what bents are serving as obstacles to achieving mission-driven goals, and what bents are optimizing those same goals?

RESOURCES

RESOURCE 1.1   BEING A GOOD BOSS

DISPOSITION	STRATEGY	VOCABULARIES
Personable	Formal and informal contacts are laced with references to a teacher's personal and professional backgrounds.	"Bill, I hear your son is going to U of M next year. Great school. Sally in the media center has a daughter at U of M. I took care of the certification problem you were having. You should get something from the county in the next few weeks."
Protective	Complaints lodged against a teacher are handled in manner that relieves the teacher of responsibility for behaviors, decisions, or methods.	"Chuck, I talked to Mrs. Larson and suggested that the comments you made were constructive suggestions for how her son could be more responsible with handing in homework. I did tell her that at times you use colorful language to describe performance issues. In the future, Chuck, I would be careful with the language you use when talking with students and parents."
Complimentary	All demonstrations of going above and beyond normal job responsibilities are praised in both private and community settings.	"Leslie, would you please stand? I want to begin this faculty meeting by recognizing the vital role Leslie played in organizing our annual holiday food pantry program. Because of her efforts, over fifty families in our community observed the holiday season with full pantries. Thank you, Leslie!"
Accepting	Out-of-the-box teaching methodologies are supported and publicly acknowledged.	"Tom, I'm sorry I was unable to catch your human chess board match. I hear the costumes worn by the students and their moves brought Shakespeare alive."
Rewarding	School community members who assume a role in achieving a schoolwide goal receive some form of compensation for their efforts.	"Bob, thank you for attending those county school improvement sessions. I am using some grant monies to compensate you for your time."
Deferential	School community members with special expertise are held in high regard.	"Before we go any further with this new reading program, let's bring in Barbara. I respect the sales representative we have, but, when it comes to reading, I listen to Barbara."
Entertaining	Throughout the school year, a variety of activities from Donut Friday to Faculty Frolics are put on to boost faculty morale.	"At our next faculty meeting, we will begin with a new program called FISH. I won't go into details now. But next month be prepared to shed some of those professional worries and just play for a couple of minutes."

RESOURCE 1.2 BENTS

TYPE	ACTIVITIES	VOCABULARIES
The builder	<ul><li>Walk-arounds/tours</li><li>Design meetings</li><li>Contractor meetings</li><li>Site visits</li><li>Bid submissions</li><li>Finance meetings</li><li>Referendum meetings</li></ul>	<ul><li>Needs assessment</li><li>Risk assessment</li><li>Timelines</li><li>Budgets</li><li>Drawings</li><li>Punch lists</li><li>Levies</li><li>District funds</li></ul>
The climber	<ul><li>Listening tours</li><li>Strategic plans</li><li>Presentations</li><li>Adoption of programs</li><li>Administrative reorganization</li><li>Conference attendance</li></ul>	<ul><li>Five-year contracts</li><li>Compensation package</li><li>Networking</li><li>District size</li><li>Signing bonus</li><li>In-state certification</li><li>The program/technique of the day (zero-based budgeting, differentiated learning, etc.)</li></ul>
The collaborator	<ul><li>Networking</li><li>Business partnerships</li><li>Learning communities</li><li>Retreats</li></ul>	<ul><li>Consensus</li><li>Stakeholders</li><li>Reconnecting</li><li>Partnering</li></ul>
The communicator	<ul><li>Newsletters</li><li>Press releases</li><li>Listening tours</li><li>Community walks</li><li>Social media (blogs, web pages)</li><li>Special events</li><li>Sponsorships</li><li>Polling</li></ul>	<ul><li>Talking points</li><li>Spokesperson</li><li>Target audience</li><li>Customer</li><li>Pitch</li><li>Publics</li></ul>

(Continued)

(Continued)

TYPE	ACTIVITIES	VOCABULARIES
The educator	• Instructional worldview • Writing/adopting curriculum • Adoption of teaching model • Staff development • Learning communities • Research • Reflection on practice	• Themes, big questions, big ideas • Pedagogies • Teaching • Facilitating • Coaching • Assessment • Frameworks • Alignment
The enforcer	• Student code of conduct • Dean's office • Referrals • Disciplinary contracts • Supervision • Police liaison officer	• Infractions • Detention • Suspension • Expulsion • Alternative placements • Zero tolerance • Surveillance
The financier	• District budget • Writing grants • Negotiating • Writing contracts • Soliciting vendors • Supervising audits • Purchasing services/materials • Bidding • Preparing financial statements	• Funding formulas • Levies • Revenues • Expenditures • Cash management • Cost projections • Insurance • Auditors • Operations • Services • Contracts • Payroll • Lowest bid
The governor	• Policies • Systems • Job descriptions • Budgets • Strategic plans • Performance reviews	• Goals • Protocols • Touching base • Timelines • Consultant • Cabinet

TYPE	ACTIVITIES	VOCABULARIES
The innovator	• Framing • Inventing/experimentation • Reimagining • Troubleshooting • Championing • Connecting	• Disrupting • Reinventing • Redesigning • Paradigms • Inflection points • Empowering • Passionate • Thinking out of the box
The technocrat	• Employ specialists/consultants • Develop merit pay systems • Establish measurable outcomes • Establish value-added measures/evaluation instruments • Establish data-driven instructional program	• Total quality management (TQM) • Data mining/data driven • Benchmarks • Accountability • Rubrics/algorithms
The technologist	• Needs assessment • Write a tech plan • Solicit vendors • Employ IT personnel • Inventory • Purchase/allocate software • District adoption of technologies • Attend tech conferences	• Infrastructure • Memory/storage • Fifth, sixth, etc. generation • Networking • Hardware • Software • The cloud • Firewalls

CHAPTER 2

....

FRIENDLY ENEMIES

*I*n this chapter I introduce "friendly enemies" of mission-driven goals and values. The comments by Principal Daniel Lopez, Truant Officer Mia Patel, Board Member Todd Rhoades, Secretary Lynn Matthews, and Athletic Director Bill Parsons all illustrate school administrators struggling with reconciling friendly institutional goals—those pursued by AGJs—with mission-driven goals—those pursued by SSLs.

Principal to Truant Officer (Pursuing Institutional Goals)	"Mia, I looked over your plan for bringing those freshman students we discussed back to school. While I appreciate the time and effort you put into solving this problem, most of the recommendations you suggest, particularly regarding starting later, modifying the physical education requirement, and substituting state-mandated course requirements, are just not within my authority to grant. Please continue to meet the county notification requirements and, if you would, ensure that data processing is coding those absences properly."
Board Member to Principal (and Response) (Pursuing Mission-Driven Goals)	"Mr. Lopez, the board would like to congratulate you on our school's performance on the SAT. This is the second year in row that the scores have gone up. Our next newsletter will highlight the rise in our SAT scores." *"Todd, while I appreciate the compliment, I don't place much value on standardized test scores. Last year when the scores came out, I shared with you the problems with using standardized test scores as a measure of our school's instructional performance. I place more value on programs, instructional methodologies, and curriculum organizations that allow students to construct their own ideas; collaborate over a problem, an idea, or a theory; and apply those understandings to real-world applications. Later tonight, I'll present a faculty proposal for the creation of an interdisciplinary program involving the four core subject areas. I hope after hearing the faculty sponsors of the program you'll consider making this program the lead in our next district newsletter."*

(Continued)

(Continued)

Principal to Athletic Director (**Pursuing Mission-Driven Goals**)	"Bill, I understand why you have asked to have your PE staff with coaching responsibilities released from seventh-period teaching responsibilities. The problem is, granting that release time for half your staff shortens the master schedule by one period. With this change, students will be unable to enroll in the classes they have registered for next year. You know I value our extracurricular program, but our educational program is what we are here for, and it will always be a priority in constructing our master schedule."
Principal to Secretary (**Pursuing Institutional-Driven Goals**)	"Lynn, cancel my observation of Mr. Meadows. I need to see how that new software package is working at Central High."
Superintendent to Principal (**Pursuing Institutional-Driven Goals**)	"Mr. Lopez, at last night's bargaining session, several of the representatives expressed concern about the state of faculty morale."

THE ENEMY WITHIN

In Chapter 1 I summarized the managerial and leadership competencies—communicator, organizer, image manager, mediator, negotiator, motivator, optimizer—that all good school administrators have mastered over their careers. While each of these qualities is essential for running a school well, strict adherence to their implementation can be a powerful enemy of the SSL. SSLs must embrace these competencies as friendly but acknowledge that they can, if allowed, become barriers to standout school leadership. What follows is a summary of the managerial values that transform these competencies into enemies and the skills employed by SSLs to keep them from becoming enemies of mission-driven goals. Each enemy is a product of managerial mindsets that value goals over vision, certainty over uncertainty, conformity over autonomy, and implementation over experimentation.

Certainty

AGJs do the managerial things well—buses arrive on time, student schedules are complete, school events are well orchestrated, and the school facility is clean and well-maintained. All of these managerial tasks are supported by systems that follow well-designed routines and are operated by well-trained staff.

The certainties of well-run organizational systems can be an enemy of instructional platforms and diverse student populations that are, by nature, uncertain. *For a school to stand out, school administrators must embrace a level of experimentation that adjusts learning environments to accommodate the ever-changing human, cultural, and social variables moving around hallways and classrooms each day.*

Façades

AGJs are skillful at communicating a positive image to the communities they serve. Through formal and informal channels of communication, they project an image of a world-class educational organization. In most main offices, any suggestion of cracks in this world-class image is quickly addressed through public relations talking points or public demonstrations of excellence. This façade can be the enemy of SSLs who value transparency. Embracing the full organizational and instructional reality means also embracing the discord that exists within the school community. Instead of focusing on projecting an image of perfection, SSLs find *and expose* obstacles that are preventing the school from truly being world-class.

> *Embracing the full organizational and instructional reality means also embracing the discord that exists within the school community.*

For a school to stand out, school administrators must author a school narrative that is transparent about the shortfalls of institutional schooling. The narrative should begin with a candid description of specific institutional structures that serve as obstacles to creating engaging learning environments. The narrative should end with specific organizational and instructional initiatives to close the gaps between institutional reality and mission-driven ideals. For an example of how an SSL might disseminate a narrative regarding a change in instructional and grading practices, see Resource 2.1.

The aversion to any form of discord within the school community is an obstacle to developing the diverse talents, abilities, and interests of its student body. The narrative titled "Three Strikes and You're Out" illustrates that committing to the development of diverse talents with full transparency might rock some boats by forcing the acknowledgment of imperfection. It also illustrates that full transparency will ultimately move a school closer to being a genuinely world-class institution.

THREE STRIKES AND YOU'RE OUT
Dr. Jim Franklyn (superintendent) and
Dr. Daniel Lopez (principal)

Superintendent Franklin:	Daniel, do you have some time? I need to talk to you about a faculty concern.
Principal Lopez:	What's the concern?
Superintendent Franklin:	I had a group of teachers visit me the other day expressing concern about what they described as your turning a blind eye to student absenteeism. Since I'm new around here, can you fill me in on the history of this matter?
Principal Lopez:	Jim, for years, some teachers have believed that student absenteeism is out of control and that I won't do anything about it. They went so far as to propose to Jamila, your predecessor, a 'three strikes and you're out' policy.
Superintendent Franklin:	They mentioned that policy. How would it work?
Principal Lopez:	They want a rule stating that any student who accumulates three unexcused absences, or a total of five excused or unexcused absences, will be automatically dropped from the class.
Superintendent Franklin:	What are your objections to the policy?
Principal Lopez:	First, from a data standpoint, our attendance rates have remained constant over the decade I have been principal. In fact, considering we serve a more diverse population than surrounding districts, our attendance rates are equal to, and in some cases better than, area rates. More importantly, I take the values we list in our mission statement seriously—above all, our commitment to be student-centered and to honor student diversity. We have a large Hispanic population in our school whose childcare issues and family obligations in other countries do result in extended absences. We have implemented a community-based program to tutor students who are experiencing attendance problems, and we've developed learning modules for students who have extended stays in other countries. I should add that I am currently revising our existing grading system to remove nonacademic values—attendance being one—from grades. Our grades would then be based solely on academic performance.
Superintendent Franklin:	While I respect your commitment to those mission-driven values and the work you have put into assisting the diverse populations we are serving, I do agree with the faculty that we need to draw a line in the sand on attendance. After all, we're preparing our children for the working world where attendance and punctuality are valued."

Principal Lopez:	Jim, with all due respect, we spent two weeks this summer writing a new school mission statement. The goals and values listed in that statement place an emphasis on nurturing the social, emotional, and intellectual growth of adolescents. I saw no language about drawing lines in the sand.
	As you can see, I feel strongly about this issue. Two former superintendents supported my effort to be faithful to the mission of this district. So, if your plan is to comply with the faculty's 'three strikes' policy, you'll have to find another principal to draw that line in the sand.
Superintendent Franklin:	Well, Daniel, most districts in the area have some defined limit to absences and consequences for exceeding that limit."
Principal Lopez:	Well Jim, as I said to you when you were interviewing for this position, we are not like most districts.

Equality

AGJs are skillful at balancing the needs and wants of the many special interest groups in their school community. AGJs are effective at distributing these wants in an evenhanded and equal manner. This equitable distribution of resources can be the enemy of an SSL who values advocacy for the priorities of a school. *For a school to stand out, the distribution of school resources must be based on what teachers and students need most, not on the wants of special interest groups.*

Bents

As mentioned in Chapter 1, AGJs are skillful at employing bents— their personal and professional interests—to solve schoolwide problems. All schools have particular problems in the organization or community whose solutions align well with one or more of the bents listed in Resource 1.2. These bents can become an enemy of an SSL when they draw attention to managerial interests and away from supervisory functions. There is only so much time in a school day. How administrators allocate their time during the day determines which schoolwide goals are being pursued and which ones are continually moved to indefinite dates in the future. Most administrative calendars are crowded with managerial functions and bents. Few administrative desk calendars are filled with supervisory functions and tasks.

For a school to stand out, school administrators must populate their daily school calendars with supervisory roles and functions: researching, observing, modeling, conferencing, facilitating, and coaching.

Cheerleading

AGJs are sensitive to how faculty feel about their work. No administrator wants to be associated with even a hint of low morale. School administrators who are intent on keeping teachers happy create a relaxed, trusting, and professional environment by developing a set of tailored managerial responses based on dispositions (see Resource 1.1). This "cheerleading" approach to high morale can be the enemy of SSLs who value *performance*. In providing a relaxed attitude towards competence, school administrators often overlook poor performance of a set of essential teaching behaviors learned in preservice training programs: knowledge of subject matter, lesson clarity, classroom management, preparation and planning, instructional delivery, assessment, and feedback. None of these essential teaching behaviors learned in preservice educational programs is neutral; they are either executed well or poorly in a school. The price paid for high morale should not be poor performance.

> *In providing a relaxed attitude towards competence, school administrators often overlook poor performance.*

That being said, SSLs do understand that for morale to remain high, faculty must perceive that the processes employed to assist a struggling teacher are fair, comprehensive, and allow the teacher the time necessary to raise their level of performance. Above all, SSLs believe that high morale and high performance are not an *either/or* choice but rather a *both/and* value. All teachers want to feel proud of being a part of an organization that values high-performing professionals. *For a school to stand out, school administrators must design performance tools, provide support systems, and be involved in the direct supervision of their instructional program to develop a school culture where teaching matters most.*

SSL TIP

My Enemy Is My Friend

AGJs have become very skilled at performing a set of managerial functions that make their schools orderly, safe, attractive, responsive, accountable, and comfortable. In devoting time, effort, and expertise to executing these managerial functions, AGJs often overlook a set of values and practices that transform a school from just *doing things right* to a school that *does the right things*—a standout school.

Every day main office administrators are confronted with a choice between pleasing a particular constituency and living up to goals and values in their school's mission statement. A school community would be comfortable with the certainties of a science curriculum that begins with biology and ends with physics. They become uneasy with a physics-first curriculum that reverses the science course sequences. A school faculty would applaud a "get tough" policy for student absenteeism, but they become uncomfortable with a "get tough" policy regarding lackluster teaching methods. AGJs fill their calendars with managerial functions and pursuits of their particular bents; this tends to please their main offices. However, those in main offices become uneasy when SSLs prioritize classroom supervision and curriculum development. School boards charge their administrative teams with developing world-class instructional programs but become guarded when asked to dismiss a tenured teacher. SSLs never forsake their mission-driven responsibilities for managerial convenience. The risks involved in upending the positive perceptions of running a school well explain why standout values and practices are often viewed by main offices as unnecessary discord that threatens the status quo.

REFLECTIVE QUESTIONS

1. Of the five friendly enemies described in this chapter, which poses the greatest challenge to advancing the educational goals and values in your school? Why is this friendly enemy posing such a challenge to mission-driven goals and values?

2. In your current administrative position, which friendly enemies are posing a challenge in performing your administrative functions? What about your particular administrative role makes these friendly enemies a challenge?

3. Describe a specific incident in your district where a friendly managerial function became an enemy of mission-driven goals and values. How did the school administration respond to this enemy?

RESOURCES

RESOURCE 2.1 INSTRUCTIONAL NARRATIVE: POSTING GRADES

SITUATION

"I called this faculty meeting to express my concern with the practice of posting student grades. In walking around the building, I found grade sheets posted next to classroom doors and inside classrooms. Several teachers told me that they use student ID numbers to conceal the student's identity. They also said that prior principals believed that it was an effective motivational tool. I will send out a more detailed memo detailing my problems with this, but I am directing all teachers to immediately stop this practice. From a legal standpoint it violates the Family and Educational Rights and Privacy Act. While it seems a simple institutional tool to report student achievement, it sets up a performance mindset ('Did I do better than others?') rather than a mastery mindset ('Have I learned the subject matter?'). As you can probably surmise from my comments, I am also not a fan of four-point grading systems or point-driven assessments. Our entire institutional infrastructure—from grading programs to progress reports—is driven by the reduction of student understandings of academic content to mathematical computations. The problem with these computations was best expressed to me by a parent at our recent parent-teacher night, who asked, 'Mr. Lopez, what does 70 percent mean?'"

STRATEGY

"In anticipation of this meeting, I sought the advice of several experts on grading and student assessment. We agreed that our current system of grading is here to stay. It is too embedded in how school communities judge student achievement. However, they did discuss several school districts that are experimenting with mastery-based grading that could be integrated into our current point- and letter-based grading systems. I've arranged to have Dr. Joel Meyers speak at our next in-service day. Dr. Meyers is a psychometrician from Northwestern who is an expert on the shortcomings of grading systems that use accumulated points and letter grades. He also will describe his work with alternative grading systems designed to clearly represent each student's unique performance."

STRATEGY

"Because I understand how firmly entrenched our institutional grading system is, I won't mandate any change in that system. But for teachers who are interested in an alternative grading system, one that reflects performance, I've made the following arrangements for the coming school year.

"First, I employed Dr. Meyers to conduct three workshops during the summer and to hold six monthly drop-in sessions for teachers interested in discussing and designing performance-based instruments.

"Second, I ordered the book *Understanding by Design* by Grant Wiggins for each faculty member. The book provides a step-by-step approach to designing lessons that align with performance-based instruments.

"And finally, I talked with Beth Johnson, our director of data management, about redesigning our current gradebook program to align with these instruments. At a workshop last year where they were the topic of discussion, Beth learned that most gradebook programs are unable to accommodate performance-based instruments. She believes that the best direction to pursue is to have teachers manually convert performance-based assessments into letter grades."

CHAPTER 3

································

WHAT IS A
GOOD SCHOOL?

*I*n this chapter I discuss the many definitions of "good schooling" offered *by members of the school community. The comments by a board member to Superintendent Dr. Abrams and by a parent, a union representative, a board member, an education specialist, a local business owner, and a college recruiter to Principal Dr. Lee all reflect these many definitions.*

Board Member to Superintendent	"Superintendent Abrams, with the state's cutback in funding, what's your plan for balancing next year's budget?"
Parent to Principal	"Principal Lee, my son is really interested in debate. Are you looking at adding it to our extracurricular program?"
Union Representative to Principal	"Principal Lee, the new curriculum standards that the district adopted will require more planning time for teachers."
Google Education Specialist to Principal	"Principal Lee, your data manager told us that you'd be interested in installing Google Workspace in your school. I'd like to talk to you about products and pricing."
Local Business Owner to Principal	"Principal Lee, we're really impressed with the students in your internship program. They have a great work ethic and get along great with our customers. My only suggestion would be to work on their writing skills."
College Recruiter to Principal	"Principal Lee, you might consider beefing up your advanced placement program."

ONE QUESTION, MANY ANSWERS

The gulf between AGJs and SSLs is revealed with the answer to this question: What is a good school? On the face of it, the question appears to be fairly straightforward. However, the answer varies wildly depending on the perspective of the person being asked (see Figure 3.1). *Board of education members* define a good school as one that is financially sound. *Superintendents* define a good school as a place enthusiastically supported by parents. *Principals* define a good school as a place that is safe and orderly. *Parents* define a good school as a place offering rich academic and extracurricular programs. *State officials* define a good school as a place that complies with legislative mandates. *Teachers* define a good school as a place that is well resourced and well disciplined. *Students* define a good school as a place with a lot of activities and venues to meet their friends. *Mission-driven goals* define a good school as one that does the following:

- has respect for individual talents

- respects divergent thinking

- encourages creativity

- creates rich and stimulating learning environments

- promotes a love of learning

- prepares students to become responsible and competent citizens

- provides venues and activity settings that allow students to pursue their passions

FIGURE 3.1   WHAT IS A GOOD SCHOOL?

CONSTITUENCY	A GOOD SCHOOL . . .
State/national legislatures (state boards of education)	• Follows state and national educational laws • Regulates school operations (school year) • Meets teacher/administrative certification requirements • Meets curricular requirements • Follows state educational standards • Adheres to school calendar
Board members	• Is financially sound • Complies with state/federal mandates • Maintains buildings/infrastructure • Enacts strategic planning (five-year plans) • Effectively manages employee contracts • Follows policy manual

CONSTITUENCY	A GOOD SCHOOL . . .
Main office	• Adheres to district/building budgets • Maintains community relations • Complies with procedures for state/federal mandates • Adheres to employee contracts • Implements board policies and procedures • Effectively plans and supervises all construction projects
Building office	• Adheres to budgets • Effectively manages systems (transportation, food service, grades/credits) • Reports on progress (report cards, transcripts) • Effectively disciplines students • Follows the master schedule (course scheduling) • Complies with state/district mandates • Maintains buildings/infrastructure • Provides robust extracurricular programs
Teachers (and unions)	• Keeps campuses safe • Supports autonomy • Provides comfortable working conditions (teacher workspaces, access to technology) • Enforces strong student code of conduct • Provides sufficient resources (textbooks, technology, media center, support staff) • Maintains small class sizes • Allows adequate planning time • Provides a competitive salary schedule
Parents	• Keeps campuses safe • Provides robust extracurricular programs • Maintains a modern/clean facility • Employs responsive staff • Employs competent staff • Offers rich elective programs • Offers advanced academic programs • Is well located
Students	• Keeps campuses safe • Employs teachers who know and care about students individually • Provides more real-world experiences (internships/fieldtrips) • Limits lectures/worksheets/tests • Offers better help with applying for college • Offers better preparation for occupations • Gives students more voice in school governance

(Continued)

(Continued)

CONSTITUENCY	A GOOD SCHOOL . . .
Colleges **(academic readiness)**	• Provides solid backgrounds in core academic subjects: math, science, social studies, English • Develops strong writing skills that include conciseness, clarity, proper grammar, and strong reasoning • Teaches effective communication in debates, discussions, and presentations • Teaches students to analyze academic texts in greater detail • Prepares students to understand and respond critically to lectures • Develops the ability to understand academic texts and lectures
Employers **(career readiness)**	• Develops critical thinking, problem-solving skills, and the ability to recognize many solutions • Encourages teamwork • Cultivates adaptability • Prepares students to prioritize/anticipate problems • Teaches evidence-gathering to solve problems • Teaches effective communication skills (presentations, negotiations, selling)
Vendors	• Utilizes the program/technique of the day • Incorporates technology • Purchases the latest instructional materials • Uses consultants

> *Each answer to the question of what is a good school makes a claim on district and school resources: time, space, personnel, and money.*

Each answer to the question of what is a good school makes a claim on district and school resources: time, space, personnel, and money. AGJs are skillful at distributing district resources that are responsive to the school community's many definitions of good schooling. Attempting to satisfy one definition of good schooling after another, however, leaves few resources for fulfilling the educational goals and practices advocated by educational professionals. While SSLs are sensitive to the differing definitions of good schooling in their communities, they remain focused on channeling resources towards mission-driven goals. To do this, they ask the right questions.

SSL TIP

Asking the Right Questions

AGJs and SSLs begin each day in their offices asking very different questions about the job and the profession. AGJs ask *what* questions:

- "What meetings do I have today?"

- "What's the timeline for the final budget submission?"

- "What's the status of the new software installation?"

- "What county office do I send this report to?"

SSLs ask *why* questions:

- "Why did I enter the profession of teaching?"

- "Why do schools exist?"

- "Why should we adopt this program?"

Without asking the *why* questions, striving to live up to the many definitions of good schooling takes precedence over the daily educational functions of school staff. Without asking the *why* questions, the purposes of schooling—why schools exist—are starved of the resources required to fulfill the educational functions of schooling.

AGJs enter and leave their buildings each day questioning the management of the varied definitions of good schooling offered up by the school community—pursuing goals based on what others want a school to be doing. SSLs enter and leave their buildings examining their role in fulfilling the educational goals and values listed in their school mission statements—pursuing the purposes of what schools ought to be doing.

SSLs shift the focus of schooling from the community's own multiple definitions of good schooling to a collective understanding of how the daily functions of school personnel will reflect mission-driven goals and achieve the purposes of schooling.

SSLs *shift the focus* of schooling from the community's own multiple definitions of good schooling to a collective understanding of how the daily functions of school personnel will reflect mission-driven goals and achieve the purposes of schooling. Figure 3.2 illustrates this shift from goals to purposes.

FIGURE 3.2   SHIFTING THE FOCUS OF SCHOOLING FROM GOALS TO PURPOSES

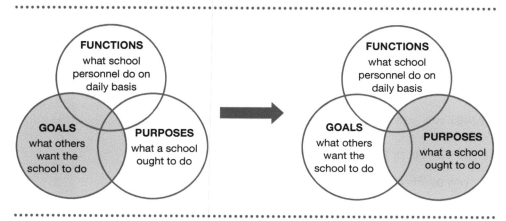

REFLECTIVE QUESTIONS

1. What are the different definitions of good schooling in your school community?

2. What definitions of good schooling govern your school's operations?

3. What definitions of good schooling would advance your mission-driven goals and values?

4. What definition of good schooling is the most difficult to implement in your school?

CHAPTER 4

....

THE ACADEMIC MIND

*I*n *this chapter I discuss the differing mindsets of managers and academics. The comments made to Principal Dr. Novak illustrate opportunities SSLs exploit to transform managerial responses into academic narratives.*

School Board Members to Principal	"Principal Novak, why are we offering Spanish courses for native speakers?"
	"Principal Novak, why doesn't our reading program place more emphasis on phonics?"
	"Principal Novak, why hasn't our school adopted the DARE program?"
	"Principal Novak, I am concerned that without a weighted grade system our students are at a competitive disadvantage in the college admissions process."
	"Principal Novak, why has a committee been set up to examine our current grading system?"

THE AIMS OF MANAGERS VERSUS ACADEMICS

AGJs are products of certification programs that concentrate on *how* to run a school well. There are few required courses in school administration programs that provide intellectual frameworks, academic concepts, or research theories that address the *why* and *what* of schooling. Even if a certification program includes a *why* or *what* course, it is typically taught by retired school administrators who lack the academic background to connect intellectual understandings to the real world of managing a school.

While all school administrators were originally trained in an academic subject, when they become administrators, the habits of thought and methods of inquiry they learned get displaced by a managerial mindset consumed with the particulars of implementing policies and putting out fires. AGJs are skillful at employing a variety of managerial tools to efficiently implement the *how* of schooling, but they often don't utilize a vast repository of academic tools to enact the *why* and *what* of schooling. Managerial minds and academic minds provide very different responses to the following four questions. The responses reflect their conceptual frameworks for enacting the *why* and *what* of schooling:

1. Why are we here?

2. How should we teach?

3. What kind of organization do I lead?

4. What should we measure?

Why Are We Here?

AGJs are excellent systems managers. The aim of a school manager is to make certain that all components of the system are aligned: budgets, personnel, materials, space, and time. In addition to tending to these managerial functions of school administration, SSLs pay attention to the philosophical and historic foundations of their profession. The aim of educational philosophers and historians is to make the case for what goals a school should be pursuing, why those goals are important, what disciplines best address those goals, and how those goals are realized in classrooms (see Figure 4.1).

FIGURE 4.1   SSLs DEFINE THE GOALS OF SCHOOLING

THE GOALS OF SCHOOLING	FOUNDATIONAL QUESTION	ACADEMIC DISCIPLINES
To educate	What is the meaning of life?	• Anthropology • English • History • Philosophy
To emancipate	Who am I?	• Arts • English • History • Philosophy • Sociology
To join	How do I effectively participate in a democratic community?	• History • Philosophy • Political science

THE GOALS OF SCHOOLING	FOUNDATIONAL QUESTION	ACADEMIC DISCIPLINES
To prepare	What do I want to become?	• Arts • Business • Communications • Computer science • Economics • Engineering • Humanities • Natural sciences • Physical sciences
To socialize	How should I behave?	• Anthropology • History • Philosophy • Sociology

How Should We Teach?

AGJs are excellent *instructional managers*. The aim of an instructional manager is to efficiently implement the components of an instructional program: allocating curricular materials, scheduling in-service workshops, purchasing instructional materials, completing teacher performance instruments, and monitoring curriculum-writing projects. In addition to tending to these functions of instructional implementation, SSLs pay attention to the pedagogical foundations of their profession. The aim of educational psychologists and curriculum specialists is to assist teachers with making collective sense of various theories of teaching and learning (see Figure 4.2).

> The aim . . . is to make the case for what goals a school should be pursuing, why those goals are important, what disciplines best address those goals, and how those goals are realized in classrooms.

FIGURE 4.2 SSLs IMPLEMENT MISSION-CENTERED TEACHING

KEY QUESTION	INSTITUTIONAL-CENTERED TEACHING THEORISTS	MISSION-CENTERED TEACHING THEORISTS
How do children learn?	B. Bloom	J. Bruner
	M. Hunter	M. Clay
	B. F. Skinner	J. Dewey
	E. Thorndike	J. Piaget
	J. Watson	L. Vygotsky

(Continued)

(Continued)

KEY QUESTION	INSTITUTIONAL-CENTERED TEACHING THEORISTS	MISSION-CENTERED TEACHING THEORISTS
What knowledge is of most worth?	W. Bennet	J. Dewey
	A. Bloom	P. Freire
	E. Hirsch	J. Rousseau
How should knowledge be organized?	F. Bobbitt	J. Dewey
	C. Judd	D. Meier
	R. Tyler	A. S. Neill
How should we assess what students understand?	A. Binet	J. Goodlad
	M. Rhee	H. Gardner
	B. F. Skinner	G. Wiggin
How should we teach?	B. Bloom	J. Dewey
	M. Hunter	M. Montessori
	B. Rosenshine	J. Pestalozzi

What Kind of Organization Do I Lead?

AGJs are excellent *CEOs*. The chief aim of a school CEO is to align building policies, procedures, and programs with institutional goals and practices.

In addition to tending to the CEO functions of school administration, SSLs pay attention to CKO (chief knowledge officer) functions. The aim of a CKO is to develop the intellectual capital of staff to actualize the educational goals and values listed in school mission statements (see Figure 4.3).

FIGURE 4.3 SSLs LEAD KNOWLEDGE ORGANIZATIONS

BUREAUCRATIC ORGANIZATIONS	KNOWLEDGE ORGANIZATIONS
Hierarchy: top-down decision-making	Flat structure and egalitarian culture
Role differentiation	Role relationships are not based on status
Impersonal environment	Autonomy and professionalism
Technical competence and performance instruments	The "logic of confidence" (close supervision is unnecessary)
Documentation, rules, and paperwork	Documentation is not the priority
Accountability focused (data, sanctions for noncompliance, benchmarks, alignment, validity, reliability, measurement psychology)	Focus is on observation and response to "intentional states" (beliefs, desires, goals, satisfactions, feelings, judgment, thoughts)

What Should We Measure?

AGJs are excellent *school accountability officers*. The aim of a school accountability officer is to report data gathered on national and state accountability instruments: standardized tests, state testing programs, schoolwide-assessment instruments, and valued-added teacher performance instruments. In addition to tending to the accountability role of school administration, SSLs pay attention to the functions of instructional leadership. The aim of instructional leaders is to work with staff to develop multiple assessment tools that reflect the right balance between quantitative outcomes that are easy to report and qualitative outcomes that are open to interpretation (see Figure 4.4).

FIGURE 4.4   SSLs DETERMINE WHAT IS WORTH MEASURING

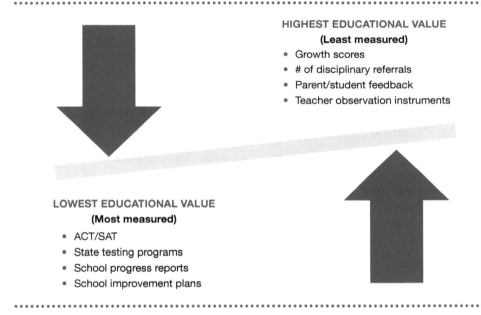

HIGHEST EDUCATIONAL VALUE
(Least measured)
- Growth scores
- # of disciplinary referrals
- Parent/student feedback
- Teacher observation instruments

LOWEST EDUCATIONAL VALUE
(Most measured)
- ACT/SAT
- State testing programs
- School progress reports
- School improvement plans

THEORY TALK

The habits of thought and methods of inquiry honored in preservice training programs rarely materialize in main offices and district conference rooms. AGJs would admit they should pay more attention to what academics say about the problems they confront—what does the research say? But when main office doors close, these administrators offer the following justifications for not paying attention to theory talk:

- **We don't have time.** The problems we face must be fixed now. We don't have time for Ivory Tower discourses on the causes and hypothetical solutions to the problem.

- **We already have the managerial tools to work with.** The problems we face are conventional. We already have tried-and-true managerial tools to fix the problem: add personnel, write a rule, change a schedule, or redesign a system.

- **We can't experiment.** The problems we face are fixable. The school community doesn't have the patience to test multiple organizational or instructional strategies that may or may not work.

- **We don't have the expertise or resources to implement theory-based strategies.** The solutions to the problems we face must employ the resources at hand. We don't have the level of expertise and organizational designs to implement theory-based strategies.

THEORY IN ACTION

School administrators' explanations for downplaying theory talk in main offices might seem to make sense in the real world of schooling, but they miss the point. These discussions are vital for cultivating the academic qualities that make SSLs stand out.

Quality #1: Academic Minds Allow for Change

All private and public practices we enact each day are governed by an idea or set of ideas—the *why* and *what* questions. Our current model of schooling is governed by a set of ideas based on learning theories developed in the early 1900s. The design of our school buildings, the age-graded classroom, the departmentalization of subject matter, the certification of teachers, and the documentation of student progress are all efficient means of achieving the institutional outcomes of standardization, compliance, and certification. Managerial-minded administrators are comfortable with operating a school system where institutional outcomes are efficiently achieved.

Academically minded administrators accept the learning principle that no idea or set of ideas is fixed. Over time, the beliefs, ideas, and practices of societies evolve. The ideas and pedagogies that governed schooling in the early 1900s have become obsolete in societies that value novelty over standardization, agency over compliance, and creativity over conformity. Academically minded administrators pay attention to current, evolving research on best practices in educational administration.

> *Academically minded administrators accept the learning principle that no idea or set of ideas is fixed. Over time, the beliefs, ideas, and practices of societies evolve.*

Quality #2: Academic Minds Solve Problems

Managerial-minded administrators employ established managerial tools to fix disruptions to organizational and instructional routines. When the problems arising in schools are simple problems involving definable variables that interact in predictable patterns, then established managerial tools work. Most problems that arise in schools, however, are complex problems involving numerous known and unknown variables that interact in unknown ways. Treating a complex problem (e.g., fighting in schools) as a simple problem with a managerial fix (e.g., enacting a zero-tolerance policy) results in the problem reappearing year after year in different forms. Academically minded administrators are not theorists who only spend time researching problems and not acting; they take decisive action after they have studied the research on the problem at hand as well as the approaches that have worked and not worked in the past. It can appear to be wasting both time and money to study these academics of a problem, but only by doing so can an SSL offer effective solutions to problems that remain puzzling in other school districts. See Resource 4.1 for a list of characteristics of an academic mind and the types of questions they might ask.

FIXING VERSUS SOLVING THE PROBLEM OF FIGHTING IN HALLWAYS

The essential distinction between a fixing and a solving approach rests with the first step in problem-solving. AGJs first turn to implementing an accepted managerial tool: a policy, a procedure, a rule, or more personnel. SSLs solve problems by first asking what we know about the problem and then basing the solution on what the research says about the problem's root cause. A good example would be the theory of unowned places as it is applied to fighting in hallways (Astor et al., 1999).

Fights and bullying are dangers to both students and teachers and create an unsafe instructional environment. AGJs would address this problem with increased penalties for fighting (more days of suspension), a program (e.g., Character Counts), or gadgets (surveillance cameras). When the first technique fails, these administrators will look to another managerial fix and start the cycle again with requests for another program or a new gadget.

In contrast, our SSL first details what is known about the problem:

- We are experiencing an increase in the number of fights in hallways.

- This violence occurs in places where teachers rarely travel.

(Continued)

(Continued)

Our SSL then looks at the research. The hypothesis of the theory of unowned places states that adolescents will refrain from antisocial activities in locations "owned by adults." In areas of the school where teachers and deans rarely go, places "owned by students," they feel free to engage in disruptive behaviors.

SSLs further study what the research says about approaches to this problem. They will learn that increasing punishment is not an effective deterrent and, in fact, is harmful to a school culture. The harsher penalties or added security guards are institutional interventions that students view as attempts to control behavior, which in turn motivates them to act out more.

Relying on the theory of unowned places, SSLs provide an organic solution that blends in with the normal operations or flow of schooling. Our SSL works with the teachers' association to have each department claim ownership of different parts of the building. Every teacher assumes supervisory responsibility for an "unowned" place in the building. By implementing a subtle intervention that puts adults near students, not only are fights prevented but there are more opportunities for students and faculty to engage in informal communications that can help establish positive relationships between teachers and students.

Quality #3: Academic Minds Connect to Larger Purposes

Managerial-minded administrators begin each school day asking secretaries what is on their calendar, thus focusing on *what* they will be doing. Academically minded administrators begin each day asking members of the school community about the purpose of their organization, therefore focusing on *why* they are doing what they are doing. The asking and answering of the *why* question of schooling keeps the community members connected to the primary reasons they entered the classroom (which were not the high pay and great working conditions).

Quality #4: Academic Minds Are Continual Learners

Managerial-minded administrators spend their day telling, allocating, and inspecting. Academically minded administrators spend their day observing, explaining, and experimenting. The latter educational functions draw administrators into processes that present new questions, new methods, and new research. To be a contributing member in this process of continual improvement requires continual learning.

Quality #5: Academic Minds Inform Each Other

During a career in district and main offices, administrators participate in countless managerial conversations and read countless managerial directives.

None of these conversations or directives, however, use the vocabularies or conceptual understandings that are grounded in academic understandings of the problems and dilemmas of schooling. The self-authoring of an academic worldview about the organization and methods of schooling occurs in conversing with and reading of academic minds outside of the purview of the standard managerial discourses of main and central offices.

WHAT DOES THE RESEARCH SAY?

All the qualities of the academic mind come into focus when members of the school community question problems or practices that they believe run counter to commonsense understandings of how a school problem *should* be solved or how a school practice *should* be executed. It would *seem* common sense that English language learners (ELLs) should be immersed in the language of their host country. It would *seem* common sense for districts to adopt programs that stress love of learning over drill-and-kill phonics-based programs. It would *seem* common sense to adopt a weighted grade system to remain competitive in the college admissions process. Decades of research on *all* the above-listed commonsense understandings of school practices have proven these practices are ineffective at best and, at worst, are harmful.

Discussions about the commonsense understandings of language acquisition, low reading scores, academic achievement, and college admissions will generate strong emotional responses from the school community. Questioning a school community's understanding of how schools *should* look and operate draws administrators into political and intellectual entanglements that question their legitimacy as school leaders.

The managerial-minded occupants of main offices who want to avoid those entanglements bypass having to explain academic understandings of a school problem or practice by simply concentrating on implementing commonsense practices, such as instituting a bilingual immersion program, employing reading coaches, publishing an annual school report card documenting student progress on standardized tests, purchasing a balanced literacy program, or converting to a weighted-grade system to be more competitive in the college admissions process.

SSLs have learned that without habits of thought and methods of inquiry that draw heavily on what the research says, there is no foundation to engage in a purposeful process of problem-solving. SSLs would be the first to acknowledge that educational research can often be conflicting, obtuse, and impractical. At the same time, however, educational research remains the primary method to evaluate the efficacy of a program and, more importantly, its potential harm to a student's social, emotional, and intellectual development.

SSL TIP

Widening the Leadership Lens

While all school administrators do share a set of common academic and practical experiences in preparing for their entrance into main offices, once there, the paths of AGJs and SSLs diverge. AGJs often don't take the time to make academic sense of the roles they perform. The *what* of the job has already been prescribed in a program, a directive, a regulation, a protocol, or a job description. The *why* of the job has already been determined by boards, governmental bodies, and central offices. AGJs were hired to implement the *how* of schooling.

SSLs accept the reality that the schools they lead are filled with countless known and unknown human, organizational, and instructional variables that will turn certain *how* questions into uncertain *why* and *what* questions. Without a collective understanding of the purposes, meanings, and activities of schoolwide initiatives, the *practical sense* of implementation is reduced to telling, allocating, and inspecting. Without the *critical sense* of self-examination, beliefs become ideologies, theories become laws, assumptions become facts, and models become routines. SSLs widen the leadership frame from solely focusing on the practicalities of implementation—the *how* of managing—to clarifying and questioning the goals and functions of those practicalities—the *why* and *what* of leading. See Resource 4.2 for a sample list of leadership lenses and the types of questions leaders with a particular lens might ask.

> *SSLs widen the leadership frame from solely focusing on the practicalities of implementation—the how of managing—to clarifying and questioning the goals and functions of those practicalities—the why and what of leading.*

1. What academic minds have most influenced you in your current administrative role? What theory, idea, concept, or practice advanced by this academic mind most resonated with you? Why?

2. Describe a situation in your school where you experienced or observed the academic mind in play. How was the academic mind treated in this situation?

3. In your current school administrative role, describe a problem or situation that you believe to be simple and a problem you believe to be complex. What particulars about these problems made them simple or complex?

4. Identify a problem or situation in your school that has gone unresolved. In your view, why has the problem remained unsolved? How would an academic mind approach this problem?

5. Identify a program or practice in your school that the research has proven to be ineffective. How has the administration responded to the knowledge that this adopted program or practice is ineffective?

6. What administrative actions in your school could be described as widening the leadership frame from solely focusing on the practicalities of implementation—the *how* of schooling—to clarifying and questioning the goals and functions of those practicalities—the *why* and *how* of leading?

RESOURCES

RESOURCE 4.1   THE ACADEMIC MIND

ACADEMIC MIND	THOUGHTFUL PRACTICE
Remains skeptical	What evidence do we have that this strategy will work?
Requires empirical proof	How do we know that this strategy is working?
Is aware of deviations from norms of practice	What is not working?
Resists efforts at simplification	What are the causes of the problem?
Is sensitive to the social context of the classroom/school	What circumstances and conditions are surrounding the problem?
Defers to expert knowledge	What does the research say?
Listens to diverse perspectives	How did you come up with that strategy?
Asks the right questions	Why do we have this problem?

RESOURCE 4.2   WIDENING THE LEADERSHIP LENS

THE LENS OF SCHOOLING	WHAT, WHY, AND HOW OF SCHOOLING
Academic sense	• Why am I here? • What do I value? • What is my instructional worldview? • What do I know about this initiative? • What theories, ideas, and beliefs govern this initiative? • What strategy should I pursue? • Does that strategy agree with the school's instructional worldview? • How will I know if we have successfully implemented this initiative?
Practical sense	• Will my school community feel comfortable with this initiative? • How should I frame this initiative to the school community? • Does this initiative pursue a valued end of schooling? • Do the theories and practices of this initiative employ familiar concepts, vocabularies, and practices?

THE LENS OF SCHOOLING	WHAT, WHY, AND HOW OF SCHOOLING
Practical sense (continued)	• Do the theories and practices of this initiative agree with the district's worldview and other instructional initiatives in the district? • Does the faculty possess the prior background knowledge to fully implement this initiative? • Do the district and school possess the organizational resources—time, material, space, and expertise—to train teachers and accommodate diverse instructional design features?
Critical sense	• What assumptions are guiding this initiative? • What am I still uncertain about? • Is the effort put into this initiative worthwhile? • Is the school community adapting to this initiative? • Are the strategies we are pursuing working? • Are the outcomes we are pursuing achievable? • Am I telling the school community members what they *need* to hear rather than what they *want* to hear?

CHAPTER 5

·····································

BEYOND MANAGERIAL TRUTHS

In this chapter I discuss how SSLs navigate around the "managerial truths" that govern main offices. The comments here reflect some of these truths— the organizational boundaries that are designed to accommodate the institutional goals of standardization, compliance, and documentation. I share how these managerial truths have come to be accepted and then discuss the lessons that SSLs have learned to work around them.

Superintendent to Principal	"Lamar, let's talk about your proposal to collapse some of the academic tracks at your school."
Union Representative to Principal	"Principal Jackson, we've noticed that many of our colleagues are being sent to workshops on cooperative learning. Will this initiative become a performance standard in our teacher evaluation plan?"
IT Manager to Principal	"Principal Jackson, our scheduling package isn't configured to accommodate your proposed interdisciplinary program offering. Is there a way to offer the program within our existing departmental structure?"
Superintendent to Assistant Superintendent	"Ed, I read your memorandum on your concerns about the new district grading policy. I sent those concerns to Olivia's office. You might also check with George on your planned reorganization of the data processing department."

MANAGERIAL TRUTHS

While academic training is necessary for framing the purposes and functions of schooling, it is not sufficient to enact those purposes in the real world of main offices and classrooms. In this chapter I consider the managerial truths that all teachers and administrators learn in their schooling careers:

- School communities believe their schools are excellent.

- Within months of entering the profession, the ideals preached in preservice programs become victims of classroom realities.

- Systems provide processes so that organizations operate consistently and efficiently.

- Chains of command ensure well-defined direction, designate responsibility, and designate clear task assignment.

Each truth identifies a belief, a routine, or a practice that controls how a school community makes sense of the schools they work in and send their children to. None of the truths are formalized in textbooks or courses in school administration. All reflect informal understandings and practices that evolve out of a system designed to accommodate the institutional goals of standardization, compliance, and documentation.

> *SSLs view these managerial truths as impediments to living up to the educational goals and values they pledged to fulfill in their preservice training programs.*

AGJs accept these as managerial truths that must be obeyed in main offices and classrooms. SSLs view these managerial truths as impediments to living up to the educational goals and values they pledged to fulfill in their preservice training programs. While they acknowledge that all change initiatives must work within the existing culture of how a school community believes its school should look and function, SSLs learn how to work within that culture while navigating around these truths.

Truth #1: Schools Are Not Broken

Wherever you stand in a school organization, you learn that administrators, teachers, parents, and students believe their schools work well. For generations, our bureaucratic model of schooling has achieved the institutional goals of safely housing large groups of students, exposing student bodies to a progression of academic course offerings, certifying the completion of academic course requirements, and providing the necessary credentials for postsecondary training and occupations.

Lodged in every school system are pockets of discontent. Some will believe there are not enough personnel, not enough time in the day, not enough support services, not enough materials, not enough communication, and/or not enough attention paid to educational goals and values. Some reform-minded administrators might mistake normal malfunctions of bureaucratic delivery systems, such as late buses, incorrect student schedules, conflicting calendar dates, or wrong textbooks, for evidence that the way we do schooling in this country is broken. However, school communities merely expect school administrators to fix these operational malfunctions in the school system, not to completely change a system that they believe works as it should. School administrators who misconstrue this discontent as calls for radical reform will lose their managerial and leadership legitimacy in the eyes of their colleagues and the school community they serve.

SSLs have taught in classrooms and worked in main offices governed by powerful organizational and instructional norms. SSLs have learned from their experiences working in school communities that any changes to organizational and classroom structures must align with the beliefs of staff, parents, and students regarding how a school should look and operate. In other words, changes cannot stray too far from the established expectations of the school community.

Truth #2: Victims of Classroom Realities

All prospective teachers enter the profession with the goal of becoming a Mr. Chips—a teacher who has mastered the art of reconciling opposing habits of thoughts and dispositions: They are intelligent, but patient with the uneducated; they are demanding, but tolerant of diversity; they are inspiring, but require mastery of the basics; they are well prepared for class, but take advantage of that teachable moment. However, within months of accepting our first teaching position, we become a version of Mr. Hand, the social studies teacher in *Fast Times at Ridgemont High*: "What are you people on, dope?" No, none of us become as pedantic as Mr. Hand, or as boring as the social studies teacher in *Ferris Bueller's Day Off*, or as cruel as Mrs. Trunchbull in *Matilda*, but very few of us are able to maintain our idealistic higher purposes and personify Mr. Chips day after day, year after year.

Figure 5.1 illustrates the cultural, institutional, and instructional forces that transform the brilliance of a Mr. Chips to the dullness of Mr. Hand. When teachers enter classrooms, they face twenty-five or more young people who want to communicate, create, assemble, and question. On their desks sit curriculum handbooks, lesson plans, and gradebooks designed to achieve a set of goals—parental, institutional, and academic—that ignore the normal social, emotional, and intellectual desires of children and adolescents. Caught between schooling goals that make little sense professionally and the developmental needs of students, teachers develop an instructional identity that is a mix of disciplinarian, entertainer, and manager.

The social context of the school and classroom will determine what that mixture looks like. In some classes, usually those teaching basic skills, the teacher assumes the role of disciplinarian and manager. In other classes, usually in advanced subjects, the teacher becomes more willing to engage students on a personal level and less reliant on the disciplinary role. The common attribute in both types of classes is the absence of the kind of social, emotional, and intellectual engagement modeled in preservice educational courses. The theories, ideas, and practices learned in preservice

FIGURE 5.1 VICTIMS OF CLASSROOM REALITIES

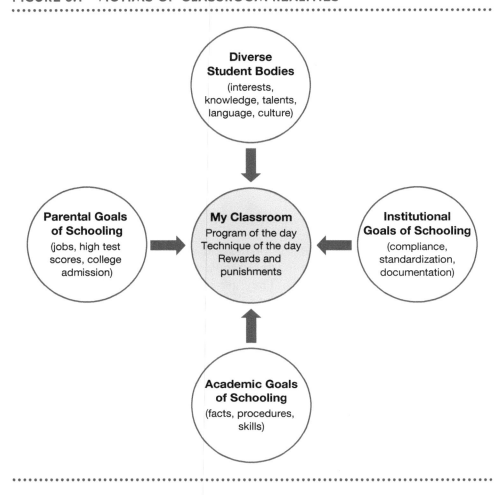

programs are replaced by a set of techniques, disciplinary regimes, and organizational structures designed to control student behavior and efficiently certify course completion.

SSLs have taught next to colleagues who have abandoned the personal, intellectual, and instructional qualities that characterize standout teachers like Mr. Chips: novel, humorous, flexible, smart, forgiving, and engaging. In place of these qualities, their colleagues have adopted routinized instructional activities—lectures, worksheets, tests, grades, homework, and textbooks—that maintain obedient but uninspiring classrooms. Here again, SSLs have learned from their classroom experiences that any changes made to classroom teaching practices must not stray too far from the familiar certainties and competence of comfortable teaching routines. In other words, changes cannot stray too far from the established expectations of the school community.

Truth #3: Staying on the Organizational Ladder

In the early days of schooling, a variety of organizational models were used. With the arrival of large numbers of immigrant children, school administrators and professional educators turned to the principles and practices of bureaucratic organizations to efficiently assemble, process, and credential the diverse mass of students knocking at their schoolhouse doors.

Schools grounded in the bureaucratic values of impersonality, hierarchies, rules, specialization, and quantification adopted rationalized instructional models that homogenized an essentially personalized function: Developmental stages became children separated by grade levels; fields of inquiry became subjects; teaching became the routinization of didactic pedagogy; different forms of communication became reading and writing; depth of understanding became breadth of coverage; mastery of knowledge and skills was reduced to a performance on a test; the intellectual significance of ideas became memorization of definitions, facts, and procedures catalogued in textbooks; and connections to the real world became rehearsed solutions to contrived real-world problems.

Figure 5.2 illustrates the organizational structures and pedagogical practices that evolved out of school systems designed to efficiently process large masses of diverse student bodies. The structure and practices pictured rest on three pillars of bureaucratic organizations: vertical division of labor, routinization of organizational functions, and centralized management. The careers of school administrators are largely determined by how well they fit

FIGURE 5.2 STAYING ON THE ORGANIZATIONAL LADDER

Top-Down Bureaucratic Organization

The State
(mandates, standards, funding)

The District
(budgets, policies, procedures)

The Organization
(chain of command, line and staff, departments)

The School
(custodian, sorting, certification)

The Teacher
(telling students what to do, collecting and grading papers)

The Classroom
(self-contained unit, periods, rules)

The Curriculum
(subjects, objectives, facts, procedures, tests)

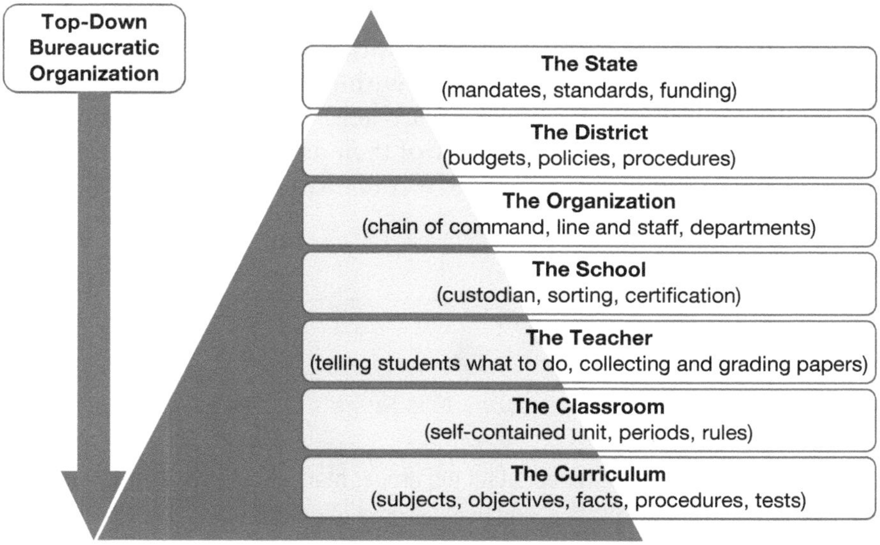

into the bureaucratic ladder pictured in Figure 5.2. Administrators climb the ladder by demonstrating to colleagues and superiors the managerial behaviors and dispositions that prove they are made of the right managerial stuff.

While school administrators enter their offices with diverse backgrounds, personalities, interests, and specialties, they all are comfortable working in offices designed to conform, comply, execute, and manage. Although these expectations would appear to work at cross purposes with educational goals that value diversity, novelty, questioning, and lifelong learning, the occupants of school offices see no disconnect between their managerial and educational roles. They believe that a well-run school will produce a world-class educational experience.

SSLs sit in offices next to colleagues who believe that bureaucratic goals and practices are advancing the educational goals and values they were taught in preservice training programs. In meeting after meeting, managerial forms—the allocation of curriculum materials, the hiring of a consultant, the administration of the state testing program, the completion of teacher performance documents, and the installation of new technologies—are understood as furthering educational functions. Here again, SSLs have learned from their experiences working on rungs of the bureaucratic ladder that any changes to normal operating procedures cannot stray too far from their assigned rung on that ladder. In other words, changes cannot stray too far from the established expectations of the school community.

Truth #4: Touching Base

Two principles govern each rung on a school's organizational ladder. First, employees assigned to each rung on the ladder know to whom they report, who reports to them, and what specific roles they are assigned to perform. Second, the performance of functions and tasks on their rung should be continually checked by the administrative position above that rung. SSLs have learned from their experiences working within bureaucratic structures that any change to organizational routines or teaching practices cannot stray too far from the certainties and competence of their assigned organizational rung. In other words, changes cannot stray too far from the established expectations of the school community.

SSL TIP

Lessons Not Taught

AGJs have become experts at orchestrating the proper managerial tools to enact managerial truths to avoid the anger, frustration, and helplessness of parents and teachers who view leadership moves as straying too far from their expectations of the school community.

SSLs have had to learn lessons to help them work around these truths by implementing changes that fall within established expectations yet move a school closer to achieving mission-driven goals.

SSLs are subjected to the same truths as their administrative colleagues. They also possess the same managerial and leadership tools to enact those truths. However, they stand out from their colleagues by being drawn to certain academic understandings of schooling that shift the focus of main offices from managerial functions to school community purposes. SSLs learn and implement the four lessons that follow that are never taught in preservice programs and rarely materialize in school offices.

> *SSLs have had to learn lessons to help them work around these truths by implementing changes that fall within established expectations yet move a school closer to achieving mission-driven goals.*

Lesson #1: SSLs Embrace New Models of Schooling

The managerial truths learned in main offices are based on 20th century models of schooling that value order and efficiency. Existing school buildings, subject matter organization, teaching methods, performance assessments, and educator certifications are all products of a system designed to prepare students to perform standardized occupational functions in bureaucratically organized industries. SSLs stand out from their administrative colleagues in understanding that schools *are* broken—that the purposes, design, and implementation of our current 20th century model of schooling are no longer useful in a postindustrial society that values critical thinking, communication, collaboration, creativity, and big-picture thinking. Whatever administrative position SSLs find themselves in, they continually look for opportunities to alter the configuration from machine-age instructional platforms to Google-age thinking and performance.

Lesson #2: SSLs Infuse Mission-Driven Goals Into the Daily Routines of Schooling

All school mission statements are expressions of aspirational educational goals that school communities value and assume are being taught in their schools. Among those educational goals most valued by a school community are developing the diverse talents, abilities, and interests of its students; imparting a set of civic responsibilities; and exchanging ideas over the kind of society we want to live in. Although these higher educational purposes of schooling—fictionally enacted by Mr. Chips—are often expressed at school community gatherings, they are rarely enacted by main offices dedicated to the efficient implementation of institutional goals that value standardization, preparation, and documentation. SSLs stand out from their administrative colleagues in understanding that school communities—teachers, parents, and students—are inspired by the

(Continued)

(Continued)

> *SSLs [understand] that a fundamental value written in mission statements is to enhance individual talent rather produce individuals with the same competencies.*

aspirational goals they believe are being pursued in main offices and classrooms. Whatever administrative position SSLs find themselves in, they continually look for opportunities to infuse mission-driven goals into the vocabularies, programs, and methodologies of the managerial functions they have been assigned.

Lesson #3: Diversity Matters

The fundamental value embedded in institutional schooling is standardization. AGJs pride themselves on their managerial competence in designing and executing systems that conform to a one-size-fits-all instructional program. Which subjects are taught, how subjects are organized, how students are assessed, and how teachers teach are all configured to be logically organized, simply measured, and efficiently reported. SSLs stand out from their administrative colleagues in understanding that a fundamental value written in mission statements is to enhance individual talent rather than produce individuals with the same competencies. Whatever administrative position SSLs find themselves in, they continually look for cracks in the organizational and instructional systems where they can honor diversity and personalize learning.

Lesson #4: SSLs Reconfigure Structures to Create Engaged Classrooms

The structure of schooling has remained the same for over a century. The design of buildings, the configuration of classrooms, the bell schedules, the categorization of subject matter, the classification of student bodies, and the organization of personnel are all products of a turn-of-the-century bureaucratic model of school that valued order, efficiency, and documentation. SSLs stand out from their administrative colleagues in understanding that any pursuit of a mission-driven value will involve a fundamental change to the entrenched structure of schooling. Whatever administrative position SSLs find themselves in, they continually seek out opportunities to reconfigure established structures of schooling to provide activities of an engaged classroom, such as the following:

- Students author their own ideas to create personal meaning.

- Students collaborate over a problem, an idea, or a theory.

- Students create real-world applications.

- Students design real-world products.

1. What lessons learned in the main office have been left out of this chapter?

2. Which managerial truths in your school have posed the greatest obstacle to realizing mission-driven goals and practices?

3. If you were mentoring a new administrator in your building, what lessons about their position would you emphasize? Why?

4. In those mentoring sessions, if you were to choose one SSL lesson to emphasize, what would it be? Why?

CHAPTER 6

....

SELF-AUTHORING

In this chapter I discuss the process SSLs engage in to develop the "self-authoring" mind. The conversation here illustrates how Principal Daniel Lopez and Truant Officer Mia Patel step out of their institutional roles and step into their self-authoring roles.

Principal Daniel Lopez:	Mia, are you aware of a group of freshman students who aren't attending school on a regular basis?
Truant Officer Mia Patel:	Yes, I am.
Principal Lopez:	What are you doing about it?
Ms. Patel:	I'm following the standard procedures of notifying and counseling truants.
Principal Lopez:	It appears from the reports on my desk that these procedures aren't working.
Ms. Patel:	I can tell you from experience that none of these measures will work.
Principal Lopez:	Well, what will work?
Ms. Patel:	Dr. Lopez, I know how to get these students back to school, but you won't do it.
Principal Lopez:	What won't I do?
Ms. Patel:	With all due respect, I know you care about these kids, but past administrators were unwilling to make the necessary changes to the school organization to accommodate the needs of these students.
Principal Lopez:	Okay, what changes would bring these students back?
Ms. Patel:	First, they don't do mornings.
Principal Lopez:	What do you mean they 'don't do mornings?'

(Continued)

Ms. Patel:	They don't do mornings. Getting on a bus at 6:30 and sitting in a cafeteria until 8:00 just won't cut it with these students. They would be willing to come to school at 10:00, but not 8:00.
Principal Lopez:	What else?
Ms. Patel:	They don't do gym.
Principal Lopez:	That's a state mandate.
Ms. Patel:	I told you that you wouldn't be able to accommodate these students.
Principal Lopez:	What else?
Ms. Patel:	They want to study subjects they are interested in, not the required courses.
Principal Lopez:	Mia, some of these required courses are state mandated. Go on.
Ms. Patel:	They don't navigate the seven-period school schedule very well. Ideally, they would be much more comfortable in some form of self-contained classroom with one or two teachers they get to know well.
Principal Lopez:	Anything else?
Ms. Patel:	Dr. Lopez, if you're really serious about this problem, I'd be willing to come on board as a resource teacher for this program. Give me a classroom in the building annex. I'll take responsibility for creating a curriculum and schedule that will accommodate the individual needs of these students.
Principal Lopez:	What about the gym and required courses mandate?
Ms. Patel:	That's a problem you'll have to solve. I'm just telling you what we need to do administratively and instructionally to bring these kids back to school.

THE MYTH VERSUS REALITY OF RATIONAL SCHOOLING

AGJs enter their offices each day prepared to complete the same managerial functions their counterparts perform in rational organizational models in the private sector. They monitor budgets, delegate tasks, write policies, examine new projects, mediate personnel issues, initiate new programs, and schedule meetings to interpret various data points. All these managerial functions assume that schools fit the profile of a rational organization.

When members of school communities look at their schools from the outside, they are limited to seeing only the shaded sections in Figure 6.1. Each shaded area *appears* to fit the profile of a rational organization. Personnel that work in schools, however, see a different schooling reality—the unshaded sections of Figure 6.1. When administrators, teachers, and staff journey beyond the shaded areas of established programs, organizational routines, and systems, they encounter the uncertainties and ambiguities arising from the numerous

ORGANIZATIONAL ELEMENT	MYTHICAL RATIONAL ORGANIZATION	THE REALITY OF SCHOOLING
Programs . . .	are based on proven theories and best practices.	
Organizational routines . . .	are repetitive, recognizable patterns of action carried out by multiple actors to control behavior and document performance.	
Systems . . .	are perfectly aligned with institutional-driven goals and values.	
Technologies . . .	are accurate, accessible, and deliver reliable data.	
Policies, procedures, and mandates . . .	are clear, consistent, sound, logical, and a guide for future planning.	are often unclear, ambiguous, and open to interpretation.
Variables in the decision-making process . . .	are known and controllable.	are unknown and uncontrollable.
Feedback . . .	is accurate and delivered in a timely manner.	is ambiguous and delayed.
Methodologies . . .	are reliable, consistent, and deliver predictable outcomes.	are uncertain, uncomfortable, and deliver ambiguous outcomes.
Inputs . . .	are quantifiable resources put into a system to produce a desired output.	are diverse talents, abilities, and interests put into a system to produce uncertain outcomes.
Outputs . . .	are the amount of a product generated by an organizational system or process.	are quantifiable outcomes measuring unquantifiable talents, abilities, and interests.

social, emotional, intellectual, and organizational factors that are swirling in and around the school facility. Some of these variables are identifiable; most are not. Some of these variables interact in predictable ways; most do not. The unshaded sections show the disconnect between the myth that schools are rational organizations and the reality of schools.

The disconnect between the myth and reality of rational schooling is exposed every year through various data points reported in the media. These include low state, national, and international test scores; bullying behavior; drop-out rates; and low student engagement levels—problems which defy rational solutions. Main offices respond to these problematic data points by doubling down on the rational methods of schooling: more personnel, more rules, more sanctions, more rewards, more systems, and/or more programs. None of these rational responses, however, significantly improves the shortcomings of institutional schooling. At some point in this failed cycle of rational problem-solving, school offices blame an uncontrollable variable or variables, such as culture, parenting, poverty, or resources, for revealing the rational model of schooling for what it is—a myth.

THE AUTHORING MIND

AGJs occupy themselves each day managing the rational components of schooling—programs, organizational routines, and systems. They ignore or implement managerial fixes for the uncontrolled variables flowing in and around their school building. SSLs, on the other hand, view these uncontrolled variables for what they are: evidence of the large gap between the institutional and human sides of schooling. No matter what the problem, SSLs step out of their managerial roles and step into an internal dialogue with their academic understandings of schoolwide problems, lessons they learned working in main offices, and the institutional realities governing school problems. Cultivating that reflective inner dialogue shifts a *managerial* mindset committed to performing assigned roles to a *self-authoring* mindset committed to owning one's work. Rather than blindly conforming to the assigned values of institutional schooling, SSLs author a personal set of goals, values, managerial functions, and methods of inquiry that question the norms of rational schooling—a personal educational worldview.

The scenario introducing this chapter illustrates self-authoring by both the SSL and the truant officer when they let go of the controlling function of institutions and embrace the aspirational goals of education. The principal begins the dialogue from within the constraints of institutional schooling by questioning the truant officer on what institutional measures she has taken to bring a group of absentee freshman students back to school. The truant officer responds in kind with a set of institutional procedures for controlling truancy. These measures amount to notifying, documenting, and counseling truants. In most school offices, the dialogue would stop at this point. Both administrators have performed their appropriate managerial roles: The principal has notified appropriate personnel of a truancy problem, and the truant officer has implemented standard truancy procedures.

> *Rather than blindly conforming to the assigned values of institutional schooling, SSLs author a personal set of goals, values, managerial functions, and methods of inquiry that question the norms of rational schooling—a personal educational worldview.*

What transpires next in this scenario is how these two school administrators step out of their institutional roles (as recounted in Chapter 2) and step into their self-authoring roles. The truant officer expresses her professional worldview—owning one's work—when she informs the principal that none of the institutional procedures that she has implemented will bring these students back to school. She then reveals her self-authoring mind by explaining to the principal how the controlling functions of schooling are serving as obstacles to bringing those students back to school.

In this scenario, the principal reveals his self-authoring mind when he presses the truant officer on how she would bring these students back to school. As the dialogue progresses, the truant officer lists the institutional obstacles to educating a group of absentee students. Several of these obstacles involve state rules and regulations as well as district graduation requirements.

Although the principal points out the institutional constraints he is dealing with, he does not stop the dialogue with an offhanded remark about the goal of developing responsible student behavior. Instead, he keeps the dialogue alive by prodding the truant officer to continue naming the institutional obstacles to solving the truancy problem on his desk. By allowing the truant officer the time and space to share her thoughts on the issue of truancy, the principal expands the boundaries of rational schooling to allow for inventive strategies to bring a group of truant students back to school.

SELF-AUTHORING IN MAIN OFFICES

No matter what venue SSLs find themselves in, at some point in a conversation they will step out of their socialized institutional role and pursue a personal set of goals and values that are at odds with managerial narratives in the room. These disruptions to routine management narratives are frequently rationalized away by a response from a colleague identifying an organizational obstacle that stands in the way of an educational goal, value, or practice. The point of these managerial responses is to remind everyone sitting in the room of the managerial roles they are expected to play in implementing the *how* of schooling.

Although the self-authoring stance of SSLs is often brushed aside, the persistent questioning of the *how* of schooling often elicits shallow conversations over the causes, outcomes, assumptions, and theories that frame a schoolwide problem or initiative. At times, these shallow conversations develop into deeper conversations about the *what* and *why* of schooling. The shift into a deep conversation about a schoolwide problem offers SSLs the opportunity to invite colleagues to participate in an examination of their own personal set of values and goals—their educational worldview.

In the case of truancy, the discussion could have been a shallow review of the standard procedures for notification, documentation, and rule enforcement. Or the discussion could have become a deep examination of *why* students are choosing to stay home from school. An in-depth conversation about the causes of truancy would encourage administrators sitting in the room to self-author a redesign of organizational and instructional routines to better accommodate the diverse learning styles of the students they serve.

Whatever schoolwide problem turns up on a meeting agenda, SSLs continually nudge their colleagues to see the connections between the *how, what,* and *why* of the problems and strategies under discussion. While the goals and structures of institutional schooling often hinder this nudging process, SSLs avoid the label of gadfly by establishing a reputation for managerial competence; they stay within the institutional understandings and acceptable norms of how schools operate.

Developing an alternative educational program to achieve mission-driven goals can include acceptable managerial norms in addition to creative approaches. For the truancy program, these acceptable norms included employing a resource teacher, allocating classroom space, and establishing different starting and ending times for the school day. Overcoming the mandate for physical education required creativity. This mandate is usually stated in terms of the number of days a week students will participate in physical activity. The mandate does not state what type of physical activity is expected, where that activity takes place, or for how long that activity will last. The mandate, then, leaves a lot of room for creating a program outside of institutional physical education regimes. The vignette about rollerblade hockey presents an example of a creative alternative to meeting the physical education requirement. The same self-authoring mindset applies to mandated course requirements. While course requirement mandates are more specific, there are numerous out-of-school academic options (e.g., correspondence courses, junior college offerings, and private tutorial services) along with in-school mainstreaming options that provide the flexibility to be creative.

> *SSLs avoid the label of gadfly by establishing a reputation for managerial competence; they stay within the institutional understandings and acceptable norms of how schools operate.*

These administrative moves can't be made without the willingness to listen to students, the courage to step out of a managerial mindset, and the resourcefulness to create learning environments tailored to meet students where they are rather than where schools want them to be. The skill to pursue educational ends without disturbing institutional means is an outcome of developing (authoring) a leadership persona grounded in disciplined understandings of the discrepancies between the practices of institutional schooling and the aspirational goals and values of mission-driven schools.

ROLLERBLADE HOCKEY
Victor Abate (superintendent) and Daniel Lopez (principal)

Superintendent Abate:	Daniel, what's going on in our fieldhouse? I walked in and saw a bunch of kids playing some kind of hockey. It's summer, there didn't seem to be any supervision, and the kids were wearing those hoodies and baggy pants.
Principal Lopez:	Oh, that's our PE program for students in TAEP (Truants Alternative Education Program).
Superintendent Abate:	How does this program comply with the state PE mandate? There was no teacher, and the students weren't dressed in our school's PE uniform. What kind of game were they playing?
Principal Lopez:	Victor, we're in perfect compliance with the PE mandate. You must not have seen the teacher, but it's Charlie Liu, one of our teacher aides who is certified in PE. He's perfect for the program. He allows the

	students to select the activities they want to participate in, how they want to dress, and the starting times for the activity. You probably saw Johnnie's own version of ice hockey, or what he calls rollerblade hockey.
Superintendent Abate:	What about the uniforms?
	In talking with these students, one reason they don't come to school is the physical education requirement. They don't like getting dressed in locker rooms and they really hate wearing a school uniform. So, in developing the program, we eliminated locker rooms and uniforms from the PE requirement.
Superintendent Abate:	Doesn't the mandate require a certain number of hours in the week dedicated to physical education?
Principal Lopez:	Actually, Victor, if we are having a problem with the program, it is getting students to stop an activity. So far, we have more than enough hours in the program to satisfy the state mandate.
Superintendent Abate:	Why can't they do this program during the school year?
Principal: Lopez:	Well, I tried. I just couldn't find a time, place, or teacher to accommodate the special needs of these students. I mentioned the problem to Charlie, who's the teacher aide in the program. He was the one who came up with the summer program idea.
Superintendent Abate:	Well, Daniel, I still have some reservations about this program. Now I'm worried about the liability issues with what you call rollerblade hockey. Those kids were really swinging at each other.

SSL TIP

Self-Authoring

A distinctive characteristic of SSLs is their aptitude to transition from the socialized mindset prevalent in institutional schooling to the self-authoring mindset required to accomplish the educational goals listed in school mission statements. There are two qualities of the self-authoring mind that stand out from the managerial mind. First is the ability of SSLs to identify how managerial goals and methods are obstacles to achieving the educational functions of their school. The second is the ability of SSLs to see their role in redesigning organizational structures to preserve the managerial means of those structures, but at the same time achieve the educational ends listed in school mission statements. Both of these abilities were on full display when Principal Daniel Lopez worked with Truant Officer Mia Patel to develop an alternative educational program that restored disaffected students'

(Continued)

(Continued)

> *A distinctive characteristic of SSLs is their aptitude to transition from the socialized mindset prevalent in institutional schooling to the self-authoring mindset required to accomplish the educational goals listed in school mission statements.*

sense of satisfaction, agency, and empowerment, enabling them to achieve what once seemed a remote goal—a high school diploma.

Figure 6.2 illustrates what goes through the mind of an SSL when they step out of their managerial role and assume a self-authoring stance. The governing thought controlling the self-authoring process is the answer to this question: What is important? AGJs answer that question with a *how* response. SSLs answer that question with a *what* and *why* response. The former response can only lead to institutional means; the latter response leads to aspirational ends.

FIGURE 6.2   THE SELF-AUTHORING MIND

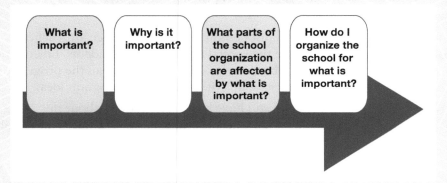

REFLECTIVE QUESTIONS

1. In your school, what *rational* approaches—policies, procedures, programs, systems, or technologies—are falling short of solving schoolwide problems? Why?

2. In your school, what explanation do administrators offer for failed efforts to solve a schoolwide problem? In your view, are these explanations defensible? Why or why not?

3. Do you believe it is rare to experience self-authoring conversations in main offices? If your answer is yes, why?

4. In administrative meetings, what prevents a shallow conversation from turning into a deeper conversation about the *what* and *why* of schooling?

5. In your current administrative role, what would a self-authoring stance look like?

CHAPTER 7

·····························

CONNECTING THE DOTS

In this chapter I discuss a key difference between AGJs and SSLs: how they think about and act upon the what, why, how, *and* who *of schooling. The following excerpts from the assistant superintendent for curriculum and instruction and the principal illustrate a managerial mindset focused on the* how *and* who.

Assistant Superintendent for Curriculum and Instruction to Faculty	"This summer I sent a memorandum to you all about our new standards-based curriculum model. You should have already received the materials to implement this curriculum and the dates for in-service training. Please pay particular attention to the assessment instruments. They require strict adherence to the protocols outlined in your test administration handbook."
Principal to Faculty	"This year we'll be implementing a new, user-friendly, data-driven student management system. It will seamlessly integrate with our existing grading system, providing us with extensive data while ensuring minimal disruption and maximum impact."

The following excerpts from Principal Kramer illustrate an educational mindset focused on the what *and* why *of schooling.*

Principal to Board Members	"Last year I worked with members of the Bilingual Department to redesign our goals and practices. An area we focused on is the high failure rates of our ELL students in academic course areas. I consulted with Dr. Ochoa, our bilingual consultant, and this year I recommend hiring native-speaking content teachers in science, social studies, and mathematics. Based on the research and conversations with students in the program, native-speaking content teachers will provide our ELL student population with access to and success in our upper-level academic programs."

(Continued)

(Continued)

Principal to Teacher	"Mr. Amin, I received a call from Mrs. Nicholson questioning her son's *D* in your class. She indicated that her son received a 100 percent on your final exam and solved your "mind-bender" problem, which I guess no one else in the class was able to solve."
	"Yes, Principal Kramer, her son did very well on the final and he was the only one in five classes to solve the mind-bender. In looking at my gradebook, I see that he lost a lot of points for not handing in homework, failing to take make-up tests, and being tardy to class. That brought his grade down to a D."
	"Mr. Amin, here's my question to you: What is the learning goal in your class?"
	"Principal Kramer, I believe that the final grade should reflect working-world values such as punctuality, following directions, and adhering to timelines."
	"It seems to me, Paul, that your learning goal values compliance over mastery of subject matter. In my mind a final grade should focus on student knowledge, not on behavior or the circumstances students find themselves in. I question the role homework should play in a grading system. As you might recall, the several articles I shared on the role of homework in classroom instruction all look upon homework as practice assignments whose primary goal is to provide a teacher with feedback on subject matter understanding, not to be used as a tool for assigning points or grades."
	"So, Principal Kramer would you have me change the grade?"
	"Mr. Amin, that's up to you. From an educational standpoint, grades should be determined by the student's most recent performance—in this case the student received 100 percent on a comprehensive final exam. A final grade of *D* doesn't reflect the level of this student's understanding of the subject matter content. It *does* reflect the implicit biases of the teacher."

PAINTING BY THE NUMBERS

A key difference between SSLs and AGJs is how they think about and act upon the *what*, *why*, *how*, and *who* of schooling. AGJs assume that the *what*, *why*, and *who* of schooling have already been established:

- The goals of schooling are legislated by governmental bodies.

- The organizational structure of schooling is determined by governmental bodies to achieve institutional outcomes, such as cost-effectiveness, credentialing, and accountability.

- The instructional delivery system is designed by professional organizations to accommodate institutional structures, such as age-graded classrooms, teacher-directed instruction, subjects, tests, grades, and rankings.

- Administrative functions are assigned by central offices to comply with governmental mandates and competently operate the organizational structure and supervise the instructional delivery system.

With the *what*, *why*, and *who* of schooling already established, all that remains for school administrators is how to successfully implement the specifications sent down to main offices from above; to do this, they paint by the numbers. Figure 7.1 illustrates the sequence of managerial tasks administrators follow when they paint by the numbers. The process is a linear one, with each step dependent on the completion of a prior step. Each step in the process is governed by the belief that the ideas, values, theories, and practices that external bodies are advocating are proven, are stable, and will interact with each other in predictable ways. The only questions asked in this process involve the mechanics of implementation: budgets, materials, personnel, space, time, and systems.

FIGURE 7.1   PAINTING BY THE NUMBERS

COLOR #1	COLOR #2	COLOR #3	COLOR #4	COLOR #5
ACCEPT THE INITIATIVE	**ASSIGN DUTIES**	**DEVELOP A PLAN**	**EXECUTE THE PLAN**	**INSPECT THE RESULTS**
• Mandate • Directive • Problem	• Offices involved • Departments involved • Services involved • Administrators involved	• Establish goals/ outcomes • Identify necessary resources (e.g., personnel, materials, expertise) • Develop a budget • Develop tasks/ flowcharts • Develop a timeline • Write policies/ procedures • Develop assessment indicators	• Establish patterns of authority • Assign personnel • Train personnel • Establish workflow patterns • Establish communication channel • Allocate resources	• Monitor newly developed policies • Monitor newly developed systems • Monitor supervisory progress • Conduct measurement • Analyze data • Identify and redesign inadequate components of the plan

FUNDAMENTAL REALITIES OF SCHOOLING

When administrators paint by the numbers, they ignore three fundamental realities of schooling and organizational behavior that doom the full actualization of the ideas, values, theories, and practices mandated by governing bodies. The first reality of schooling is that all changes to schooling routines originate from somewhere. The authors of these changes are directing administrators and teachers to adopt a specific set of beliefs, values, theories, and methods. While research may reflect current understandings of teaching and learning, these understandings may be widely divergent from the beliefs, values, theories, and methods of the school community they aim to transform. An administrator painting by the numbers never considers the connection between the managerial *how* and the educative *what*, *why*, and *who* of particular understandings and practices of teaching and learning.

The second reality of schooling is that all schools present the appearance of a well-ordered environment: Bells ring on time; students sit listening to teachers talk, completing worksheets, and taking tests; grades are entered in gradebooks; credits are issued for completed courses; and students advance through an ordered sequence of academic subjects. Alongside the institutional world of a smoothly operating school machine—where AGJs paint by the numbers—exist mission-driven goals valuing the diverse talents, interests, and abilities of the children and adolescents they serve. An administrator painting by the numbers never appreciates the connection between the conformist demands of institutions and the individualities of teachers and students (see Figure 7.2).

FIGURE 7.2   DEEP-SEATED CONTRADICTIONS OF SCHOOLING

Institutional	Inspirational
(Conformist demands)	(Individualities)
School Centered	**Child Centered**
(To follow directions)	(To develop agency)
Uniformity	**Diversity**
(To accurately classify)	(To develop a sense of belonging)
Preparation	**Lifelong Learning**
(To develop skills)	(To develop an interest)
Replicative Thinking	**Critical Thinking**
(To recite information)	(To develop knowledge)

> *An administrator painting by the numbers never appreciates the connection between the conformist demands of institutions and the individualities of teachers and students.*

The final reality of schooling is that all main offices are subject to the political pull of a variety of special interest groups desiring access to limited school resources. Administrators respond to these special interest demands with a mixture of "split the difference" fixes. Each fix, however, draws resources away from the central mission of schooling—educating—and muddles the answers to the *what*, *why*, and *who* of schooling. A leader painting by the numbers pays little attention to the purposes of schooling.

CONNECTING THE DOTS

With these fundamental realities of schooling in mind, SSLs view the *what*, *why*, *how*, and *who* of a change initiative with a different set of assumptions than AGJs. SSLs believe:

- The goals of schooling are many and varied.

- The organizational structure of schooling is determined by central and building administrators attempting to accommodate agreed-upon educational goals: flexibility of mind, openness to the understanding of others, disciplined thinking, and lifelong learning.

- The instructional delivery system is designed by teachers and administrators to develop the diverse interests, talents, and abilities of children and adolescents.

- The administrative functions are assigned by building-level administrators to enact a school's educational goals and agreed-upon teaching methodologies.

Each of these differing assumptions allows for varied interpretations of the *what*, *why*, *how*, and *who* aspects of a change initiative. Introducing multiple interpretative frameworks into the change process muddles the *how* of implementation. AGJs try to avoid any risk of this muddling by painting by the numbers. However, ignoring the differing interpretations of a change initiative will doom the full enactment of the goals, values, theories, and practices of that initiative.

SSLs untangle muddled implementation—the fate of most change initiatives—by treating the *how* of implementation as secondary to an educative process of establishing connections between purposes and practices. In the narrative titled "Muddling the State Testing Program," Superintendent Marie Hart calls an urgent meeting to discuss a new state testing program with Principal Jacob Kramer and English Department Chair Sean Finney. Superintendent Hart proceeds to muddle the implementation. Later, Principal Kramer and Mr. Finney discuss how they will untangle this muddled implementation.

MUDDLING THE STATE TESTING PROGRAM
Marie Hart (superintendent), Jacob Kramer (principal),
and Sean Finney (English Department chair)

Superintendent Marie Hart:	Thank you for coming in on such short notice. We need to get going on preparing our students to do well on the new state testing program. I've ordered test preparation packages for the upcoming program. These materials come from the same company that publishes the SAT test preparation booklets. I talked with representatives from the company. After analyzing the state testing formats, they've written materials that will make our students comfortable with these formats and offer some tips on test-taking. Sean, please work with your teachers to introduce these materials into your daily lesson plans. At the board meeting next week I'll discuss the importance of scoring well on these tests and let them know what we're doing to prepare our students for them.
Principal Jacob Kramer:	Marie, the English Department, under Sean's direction, has just completed a two-year curriculum project that redesigned how we teach reading and writing. Just last year the board allocated the monies for the materials necessary for the full implementation of the new curriculum. Sean, what are your thoughts on using these test preparation materials?
Department Chair Sean Finney:	Dr. Hart, let me express my concern with these materials. First, students learn fewer reading and writing skills and less content when test-prep materials edge out time devoted to teaching those skills. Secondly, as Jacob just said, I've worked for the last two years with the teachers in my department to design a curriculum that offers a coherent and researched path to careful, critical reading and clear, logical writing. I'm bothered by your assumption that our curriculum is superfluous and that in lieu of it students need a crash course on how to take the kind of test the state provides.
Superintendent Marie Hart:	"I have great respect for both of you. Sean, I know you have a deep background in the teaching of reading and writing, but I must insist on these materials becoming a part of classroom instruction. I'll leave it up to you on how you get this done, but you will get it done."

THE UN-MUDDLING OF THE STATE TESTING PROGRAM

(A Conversation After the Meeting)

Sean Finney (English Department chair) and
Jacob Kramer (principal)

Department Chair Finney:	"Well, Jacob, where to go from here? I've spent the last two years working on changing how teachers in the department think about and teach writing. I know you've observed quite a few classes and likely agree with my assessment that most of our teachers have finally bought into the redesigned approaches to teaching reading and writing. I can't ask them to throw all of that learning and commitment out the window."
Principal Jacob Kramer:	"Sean, we are *not* throwing away the progress you've made with your department. I see no harm in allocating some time for students to take some practice exams. I believe it will be helpful for our students to have some familiarity with the structure of the test. Beyond that, though, keep doing what you are doing. Let me handle the blowback."

Teachers are more prone to adopt foreign theories and practices when they believe they are working with their colleagues to achieve educational ideals or aspirational goals. SSLs also address the practicalities of implementation by providing the necessary resources—time, materials, space, and expertise—to connect abstract theories to classroom realities. Guest speakers, conferences, and workshops expose teachers to educational ideals. Hiring coaches, granting release time, funding summer courses, redesigning curriculum, and orchestrating learning communities immerse teachers in a theory–practice loop.

The fundamental difference between connecting the dots and painting by the numbers is the desired outcome of each process. If the desired outcome of the change initiative is to implement the *forms* of a change

> If the desired outcome of the change initiative is to fully enact the substance of a change initiative, then connecting institutional realities to educational values and methods–connecting the dots–will redefine the fundamental realities of schooling.

initiative—distribution of materials, training, and documentation—then painting by the numbers will satisfy central offices. If the desired outcome of the change initiative is to fully enact the *substance* of a change initiative, then connecting institutional realities to educational values and methods—connecting the dots—will redefine the fundamental realities of schooling.

THE *HOW* OF CONNECTING THE DOTS

Figure 7.3 is a big-picture depiction of the components of connecting the *what*, *why*, *how*, and *who* of a change initiative. It provides a summary of the managerial and leadership moves that SSLs orchestrate to assist teachers in making collective sense of the differing community, organizational, and instructional realities they are being asked to change. The arrows represent a continuing process of connecting purposes to practices. The process continually moves back and forth between the aspirational goals of purpose and meaning (what we believe and who we are) and the practicalities of implementation (how we enact). The question remains: How do SSLs connect the change initiative dots? The six strategies and tactics summarized here describe how SSLs connect purposes to practices.

FIGURE 7.3   CONNECTING THE DOTS

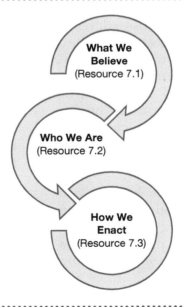

STRATEGIES SSLs USE TO CONNECT PURPOSES TO PRACTICES

- Start with a story.
- Know your systems.
- Gather your resources.
- Gather your allies.
- Put needs before wants.
- Show up.

Start With a Story

At the beginning of each school year, administrators stand on auditorium stages and announce the change initiative of the day. The opening agenda in Figure 7.4 represents the established managerial presentation of a new change initiative. The first part of the agenda is aspirational in tone: Values such as *excellence*, *new beginnings*, and *world class* are declared to be core beliefs in the district. Administrators point to new structures, new initiatives, new awards, and new data that prove the existence of the values that are printed on school letterheads and in publicity pamphlets.

FIGURE 7.4 SCHOOL DISTRICT 86 OPENING DAY AGENDA: "WHERE EXCELLENCE IS A TRADITION"

Dr. Emily McGrath (superintendent)
"Where Excellence Is a Tradition"
Dr. Ben Ford (principal)
"A New Beginning"
Ms. Laura Hunter (assistant superintendent of data, assessment, and research)
"Data-Driven Teaching"
Dr. Walter Zimmer (assistant superintendent for instruction)
"Data-Driven Decision-Making"
• Distribution of materials • Benchmarks • Workshop schedule • Timelines
Dr. Angela Crawford (consultant, Pearson Education Limited)
"Looking Inside a Data-Driven Classroom"
PowerPoint Presentation

The second part of the agenda is operational in tone: Values such as *data-driven pedagogies, standards, annual yearly progress, mandates,* and *test scores* are essential functions in the district. Administrators point to new programs, new administrative positions, new benchmarks, and new systems proving the necessity of paint-by-the-number managerial scripts: telling → allocating → training → inspecting.

Seated in the back of auditoriums under darkened lights, teachers quickly turn their attention from these declarations of excellence to the materials they removed from their mailboxes: class lists, room assignments, subject assignments, and lists of materials. As teachers look through the classroom realities they will confront the next day, the comments whispered here marginalize the educational and organizational ideals being promoted on stage:

- "We need to talk about Harry Larson. I've got him for algebra."
- "I thought we did that data-tracking program a couple years ago."
- "I wish they would put some excellent paint on my classroom walls."
- "We are going to miss Dr. Francis this year. She was the only one that knew what was going on around here."
- "No way am I showing up for a Saturday workshop."

These comments conclude with the question all teachers in the country ask at the end of their opening day programs: "Where are we going for lunch?"

The whispered comments circulating around the rears of auditoriums expose a chief shortcoming of paint-by-the-number narratives: They don't tell a story. The agenda in Figure 7.4 lays out a plan of action for painting by the numbers. Left out of the presentation is why teachers should care about data-driven instruction and what data-driven teaching will look like inside their classrooms.

To halt the whispering and turning of pages in the backs of auditoriums, officials on stage must author an opening day narrative that is understandable, emotional, and memorable. A good story inspires people to join together in solving an agreed-upon problem that is obstructing a valued end of schooling. Mere talk of excellence and program implementation lacks all these qualities.

Figure 7.5 illustrates the process that an SSL engages in to author a narrative that connects the *what, why, how,* and *who* of change initiative. SSLs craft their narrative around a schoolwide problem that teachers feel is vital to their success in the classroom. That problem is brought alive with a well-known anecdote, a picture, a number, or an encounter that captures the attention of teachers. In the case of a poorly designed bilingual program, an SSL admits to the program's shortcomings, places the blame on his leadership, and ends his narrative with a description of an encounter with an ELL parent that associates a valued end of schooling—embracing diversity—with the goals and content of the new program (see the narrative titled "Is This Really My Daughter's School?").

FIGURE 7.5 AUTHORING AN INSTRUCTIONAL NARRATIVE

THE SITUATION
(What is wrong?)
What is the problem?
How did we get here?
Where are we going?

CAPACITY	STRATEGY
(Can we do this?)	(How will we do this?)
• Personnel	
• Time	• Theories, ideas, practices
• Space	• Scope of change initiative
• Materials	• Level of faculty expertise
• Expertise	• Curriculum design
• Systems	

NARRATIVE
(How do I persuade?)
• Metaphors
• Analogies
• Stories
• Exemplars

"IS THIS REALLY MY DAUGHTER'S SCHOOL?"

Principal Jacob Kramer: "At the end of last year, a group of teachers sat in my office and asked me the following question: "Principal Kramer, how do you expect us to teach our subject matter content to students who can't speak English?" Based on the increased enrollment in our bilingual program, the question asked by that group of teachers was a valid one, and one to which, quite frankly, the administration had not provided an adequate answer. If we are to live up to our commitment to diversity and provide our Spanish speakers with a quality educational experience, this is a question we must answer.

(Continued)

(Continued)

"After that meeting, I called together teachers from our Bilingual Department and personally had extended conversations with them and with numerous professors in the field and directors of bilingual programs in the area. These extended conversations made me realize that our bilingual program had several structural flaws that hindered our staff's ability to effectively educate our ELLs. To put it bluntly, our bilingual program as currently organized could be viewed as a prime example of educational malpractice. This malpractice was no fault of the teachers in the program—it was the fault of leadership, which begins in my office.

"Over the summer I brought together members of a nearby bilingual department, the supervisor of District 96's bilingual program, a consultant from our local cooperative specializing in bilingual programming, a former student in our program (who recently graduated from Saint Xavier's teacher's education program), and Gabriela Ramirez, our community representative on the administrative council. In meetings throughout the summer, we redesigned the organizational systems and adopted pedagogical practices to achieve four goals. First, we wanted to maintain and develop the language of our ELL students. Second, we wanted to support our ELL students to do well in advanced academic courses when they possess the academic background from their native countries to do well in those courses. Third, we sought to reduce the time that ELL students spend in our bilingual program. And fourth, we wanted to provide teachers in our academic content areas with teaching strategies designed to develop the academic vocabularies of the ELL students in their classes.

"To that end, we have redesigned the curriculum for academic courses in science and mathematics to be conducted in a student's native language by teachers fluent in that language. The curriculum is structured to decrease the time that ELL students need to spend in our bilingual program. We developed a training program to provide teachers in our academic content areas with teaching strategies specific to the ELL students in their classes.

"When the year gets underway, I'll send you all a copy of the proposal I submitted to the Board of Education regarding the redesign of our bilingual program. I will also send out monthly progress reports on the status of the new program.

"This summer I gave a school tour to an enrolling student and her parents. As we walked around the school, I noticed that Mom was crying. When I asked her if anything was wrong, she answered in Spanish and her daughter translated: 'Is this really my daughter's school?' It seems the mother was overwhelmed with gratitude and amazement that her daughter would have an education that honored her home language, honored her existing knowledge, and provided trained teachers who had the ability to help her child become proficient in academic English in record time. The mother's emotional response left me standing in the middle of the social studies hallway reminded of why we all entered this profession: to make every student feel at home in their school."

Although the goal of an instructional narrative is to communicate a sense of urgency about a schoolwide problem, the narrative must include enough program details to persuade teachers that program strategies are sound and will be fully funded. The explanation of the bilingual program redesign in this narrative includes several paragraphs devoted to the theories that will guide the program—maintaining native language and academic subjects conducted in native language—and how those theories will look in practice. As seen here, SSLs elaborate on the recurring themes of urgency, of inquiry, of preparing, and of capacity—connecting the *what*, *why*, *how*, and *who* of schooling.

Know Your Systems

All organizational and instructional systems in schools are designed to support and advance institutional goals and values. The failure of change initiatives to gain traction in schools is usually due to the disconnect between the theories and practices of the change initiative and the organizational systems already in place. The essential component of implementing a change initiative is aligning the *what*, *why*, *how* and *who* of the initiative with a school's organizational systems.

Figure 7.6 illustrates the managerial and leadership tasks that SSLs orchestrate to connect the dots of systems. The successful redesign of a school's bilingual program involves the alignment of the following organizational and instructional systems:

- The personnel system will employ qualified native speakers in targeted subject matter areas.

- The professional performance system will reflect the proper application of ELL pedagogical techniques.

- The staff development system will train teachers in the application of proper ELL pedagogical techniques.

- The course-sequencing system and staff assignments will accommodate the proper placement of ELL students.

Each of these systems will be adjusted to accommodate the particulars—theories and practices—of a proposed change initiative.

Main offices that paint by the numbers would avoid disrupting any of these established organizational and instructional systems. As long as the forms of the change initiative are complied with—allocation of materials, training, and documentation—then the substance of the change initiative—theories and practices—are negotiable. As an example, the state testing program is delivered with the proper packaging test booklets and answer sheets and a detailed outline of the *forms* of the program: who can administer the test, when the test can be administered, where the test will be administered, how

FIGURE 7.6 SYSTEM ALIGNMENT

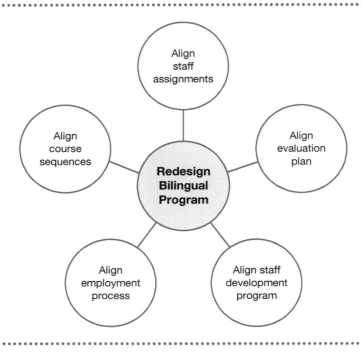

the test will be monitored, and where to send the completed tests. While administrators busy themselves with these managerial details of test administration, the *substance* of the testing program—whether the tests actually measure mission-driven goals—receives little or no attention.

SSLs do not proceed with a change initiative until they are certain that all organizational systems can be arranged in a manner that maintains the substantive integrity of the change initiative.

Gather Your Resources

Figure 7.7 illustrates the managerial and leadership tasks SSLs orchestrate to connect the dots of resources. All change initiatives recommend a mix of resources necessary for the full enactment of the initiative. In general, the authors of these initiatives ask district offices to make investments in resources. The requested list of resources is typical for full enactment of a change initiative and may include the following:

- a consultant (preferably full time)

- a training regime requiring weekly release time for targeted teachers

- a summer curriculum writing project involving all the targeted teachers and the consultant for a prescribed number of hours

- space within the building reserved for team meetings
- a master schedule designed around common planning times for targeted teachers
- a technologies and software budget aligned with program theories and practices
- a continuing agreement to purchase updated materials and technologies

Main offices that paint by the numbers skip the sections of the program manuals titled "Fully Enacted Programs" and proceed to pages titled "Goals," "Standards," "Effective Practices," "Sample Lessons," and "Fillable Templates." SSLs, however, do not proceed with a change initiative until they are certain they can afford and acquire all the resources listed in the section titled "Fully Enacted Programs" (see Resource 7.3).

FIGURE 7.7 GATHER YOUR RESOURCES

Gather Your Allies

At some stage in a change process, the managerial tools for supporting the enactment of theories and practices must be connected to teachers and staff members. In main offices that paint by the numbers, the connections between the contents of the change initiative and the roles faculty and staff will assume are prescribed in the initiative: manager, supervisor, learner, recorder, mentor, or liaison. While filling these perfunctory roles will satisfy the shallow representations of theories, ideas, and practices, they will not foster the type of professional commitment necessary to enact true versions of an adopted change initiative.

The source of the professional commitment required to enact the substance of a change initiative are peer groups within the school that see value in the goals and practices they are being asked to enact in their classrooms. SSLs do not proceed with a change initiative until they have developed a coterie of teachers and staff committed to the goals, beliefs, and practices of the initiative.

Put Needs Before Wants

Those who announce new programs from auditorium stages want administrators and teachers to adopt theories, concepts, and practices that will substantively change how administrators lead a school and how teachers teach in classrooms. They want administrators and teachers to abandon comfortable working routines and adopt foreign theories, concepts, and practices. Such a significant shift in administrative and teaching dispositions, beliefs, and practices will require school staff to expend immense amounts of emotional and physical energy. They cannot waste this energy on day-to-day concerns over building safety, lack of resources, rundown classrooms, poor delivery of services, or an antagonistic administration. An SSL makes certain that before asking their colleagues and teachers to self-author a new instructional persona, they have satisfied their staff's basic human and professional needs. Among the most important of these needs are building safety, building cleanliness, adequate supplies and services, efficient systems, a pleasing physical environment, and a supportive administration.

> *An SSL makes certain that before asking their colleagues and teachers to self-author a new instructional persona, they have satisfied their staff's basic human and professional needs.*

Show Up

Nothing speaks louder to teachers about the importance of a change initiative than seeing school leaders' personal enthusiasm and active involvement in the programs they announce from auditorium stages. School administrators whose only connection to a change process is making periodic announcements, delegating supervisory tasks, authorizing the purchase of resources, and sending out progress reports send a clear message to teachers that the initiative will be forgotten by Thanksgiving break.

SSLs believe that "showing up" sends the clear message to teachers and staff that they have a personal stake in making certain that the initiative is successfully enacted. Figure 7.8 illustrates the managerial and leadership roles that SSLs orchestrate to demonstrate that they are showing up. SSLs do not proceed with a change initiative until they are certain they have the time to listen, the expertise to educate, the skills to participate, and the authority to adapt.

FIGURE 7.8   HOW SSLs SHOW UP

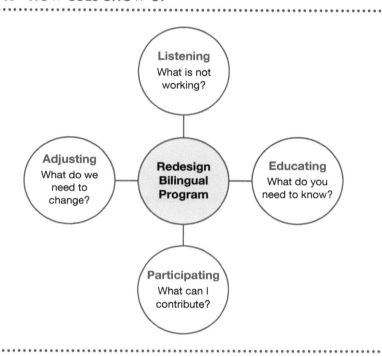

COLLECTIVE SENSEMAKING

In this chapter I have presented the key variables—dots—that school administrators must connect when adopting a change initiative. Although the type, number, and complexity of the dots will vary from district to district, the common pattern that emerges from the change process is the ability on the part of school administrators to translate abstract theories of teaching and learning into concrete teaching practices. Figures 7.1 to 7.5 presented in this chapter illustrate the many layers involved in making collective sense of programs formulated far from the everyday realties of classroom teaching.

AGJs treat the sensemaking process as merely a managerial matter of connecting various organizational variables to achieve an institutional outcome. SSLs view collective sensemaking as an educational process in which teachers and administrators structure unfamiliar theories and practices into workable classrooms routines. Figure 7.9 illustrates the mix of sense-making functions that SSLs orchestrate each day to make practical sense of a change initiative.

FIGURE 7.9   CONNECTING THE SENSEMAKING DOTS

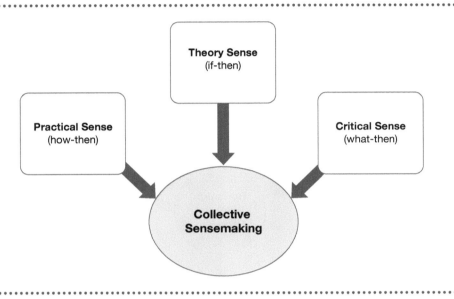

In the day-to-day supervision of classroom situations, SSLs will use different mixes of functions to assist teachers with making collective sense of a new change initiative. At times SSLs may need to work with teachers in making sense of the theories governing a new change initiative. At times they may need to apply a practical sense of view to reinterpret the applications of a new change initiative to better align with their faculty's academic and classroom experiences. And sometimes SSLs may need to consider a new initiative in a critical sense to be truthful about what is working and what is going wrong. At all times SSLs position themselves in teacher workspaces to assess which sensemaking functions are working and which require the additional educative, supervisory, or managerial tools to address misrepresentations, frustrations, or incompatibilities with the change initiative.

SSL TIP
Connecting the Dots

A unique quality of SSLs is their capacity to move from the socialized mind of institutional schooling to the self-authoring mind described in school mission statements. There are two qualities of the self-authoring mind that stand out from those of managerial minds. First is the disposition of an SSL to assume a critical stance towards the institutional norms governing the offices they occupy. The second is the ability of the SSL to assume a specific role in redesigning organizational structures that both preserve managerial means and, at the same time, achieve educational ends.

Figure 7.10 illustrates what goes through the mind of an SSL when they step out of their managerial role and assume a self-authoring stance. The recurring theme in the self-authoring process is solving transformational challenges—connecting the purposes of schooling to the strategic and tactical implementation of programs. AGJs stay within their managerial stance, where their sole focus is tactical—painting by the numbers. SSLs continually step into a transformational stance, where their sole focus is connecting purposes to practices.

FIGURE 7.10   HOW SSLs CONNECT THE SELF-AUTHORING DOTS

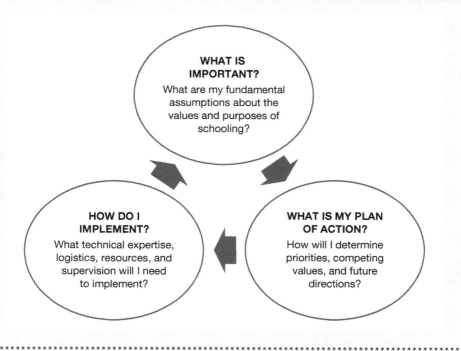

1. In thinking about your school's mission statement, do you see any contradictions between mission-driven goals and the values and current practices in your school? If so, why do you believe these contradictions exist?

2. If gaps exist between mission-driven goals and school practices, has your administrative team addressed these gaps? If not, why not?

3. As you think about the meetings with your administrative team, what purposes, values, and beliefs are expressed by members of the team?

4. If you were assigned the job of presenting to your faculty the goals and practices of a new change initiative, how would you design the presentation to inspire staff instead of leaving most in the auditorium just wondering where they will eat lunch?

5. This chapter describes the six "dots" that must be connected to ensure the successful implementation of a change initiative: a powerful narrative, knowing your systems, gathering your resources, gathering your allies, putting needs before wants, and showing up. As you think about change initiatives in your school, which dots do you believe have been connected and which are still left disconnected?

RESOURCES

RESOURCE 7.1   WHAT WE BELIEVE

THE VALUE	DEFINED	ORGANIZATIONAL RESPONSE
Intellectual (How do we examine life?)	True intelligence is not knowing all the answers but knowing what questions to ask.	Teaching matters.
Knowledgeable (How do we explain life?)	A professional knows the *what*, *why*, and *how* of their subject.	Competence matters.
Respectful (How do we treat each other?)	Children learn best in environments where diverse talents, abilities, and interests are known, respected, and nurtured.	Relationships matter.
Skillful (How do we enact our values?)	Successful organizations do the small things well.	Execution matters.
Thoughtful (How do we solve problems?)	Beliefs, judgments, and actions are supported by reasons and the evidence they provide.	Reasoning matters.

RESOURCE 7.2   WHO WE ARE

SCHOOL FUNCTION	BELIEFS
Teaching	Teaching is what matters most in schooling.
Learning	Learning is the full engagement of a child's social need to be known, the emotional need to be interested, and the intellectual need to understand the world around them.
Performance	Performance is providing quality educational experiences based on students' expectations and needs.
Professionalism	Professionalism is a reflection on practice.
Collaboration	Collaboration is intelligent participation.
Execution	Execution is doing small things well.

WHAT WE PAY ATTENTION TO	WHAT WE DO
Details	Appropriate materials and expertise have been acquired and deployed.
Alignment	Adopted theories and practices align with the school's instructional worldview.
Authority	Personnel charged with the enactment of a change initiative possess the relevant knowledge and experience to orchestrate the process of collective sensemaking.
Normalization	Managerial tools (e.g., budgets, policies) and organizational systems accommodate adopted theories and practices.
Permanence	Instructional and supervisory documents and procedures accurately represent the theories and practices of adopted program initiatives.

CHAPTER 8

....

DISCIPLINED TALENT

*I*n this chapter I discuss why the development of talent in the teaching pro-
*fession rarely extends beyond the hiring and induction of new teachers.
The conversation excerpts here illustrate the cultural, institutional, and legal
barriers to developing the individual strengths of a teaching staff.*

Teacher to New Teacher	"Alexis, don't worry about your first observation. Like I told you, just make sure you do all Hunter's seven steps. That's all they look for."
Teacher to Principal	"Principal Davidson, why didn't I receive a superior rating this year?"
Assistant Principal to Principal	"Steve, I know I'm running late on my teacher observations. I've been working on those changes to the budgetary calendar. I'll have the remaining write-ups completed within the contract timelines."
Union Representative to Principal	"Principal Davidson, would you consider transferring Ms. Jane Ferguson to the media center?"
Board Attorney to Superintendent	"Superintendent Riley, I reviewed Jim Clark's personnel file. I understand your concerns regarding his performance in the classroom. Certainly off-color humor, along with deviations from the prescribed curriculum, are serious matters. The problem we have with any disciplinary action is that past performance reports rated Mr. Clark as a superior teacher with numerous descriptors indicating that his teaching is 'creative,' 'engaging,' and 'magical.'"

INSTITUTIONALIZED TALENT

Of all the organizational and leadership qualities that SSLs possess, one skill that stands out from the others is how SSLs handle talent. All administrators would agree on the importance of managing talent. To stand out they must delve more deeply into this important aspect of leadership. The disappearance of talent development from main offices is the result of four beliefs about the nature and utilization of talent in schools:

1. All teachers are talented.
2. Some teachers have talent, but most don't.
3. Certification is enough.
4. The ability to coach is a bonus.

All Teachers Are Talented

One value highly honored by teachers is the egalitarian nature of their profession. Faculties are resistant to attempts by administration to introduce any form of employee stratification in their schools. Although teaching styles are many and varied, teachers firmly believe that all teachers possess unique talents and equal abilities that should be honored by those in school offices.

Some Teachers Have Talent, but Most Don't

While teachers may not admit to gradations of talent amongst themselves, administrators *do*. Most believe that these gradations are the result of an innate quality that some teachers have, but most do not. They believe that talent cannot be developed—only discovered.

Certification Is Enough

The managerial norms governing the staffing of schools employ institutional vocabularies to define talent: degrees, certifications, licenses, or valued-added scores. When a teaching position becomes available in a school, most administrators see it as their job to match a candidate's institutional qualification to a particular grade, subject, or specialty.

The Ability to Coach Is a Bonus

An institutional norm all school administrators confront is the role that extracurricular activities play in staffing their schools. Parents often pay little attention to what happens in classrooms, but they pay a lot of attention to what happens in extracurricular venues. While parents are willing to give some slack to less-than-talented teaching, they have little patience for less-than-talented coaching. This school community value dominates the staffing process, and the central question becomes "Do we hire a teacher or do we hire a coach?" The budgetary reality is that these positions—teacher and coach—often cannot be separated. Those in main and central offices see no problem with combining both job functions. They assume the skills needed for teaching and coaching are the same. In practice, the skill set of teaching an academic subject is quite different than the skill set used on the playing field. Cases of individuals who are talented in performing both functions—teaching and coaching—are rare.

These four beliefs have all but eliminated the consideration of talent as an essential component of what makes a school stand out. Administrators who are busy managing the functions of the personnel system in their school (see Figure 8.1) miss the opportunity to have meaningful discussions of talent. Each function is governed by managerial protocols that prescribe in detail a series of tasks that an administrator must complete in order to comply with district and school personnel policies and procedures.

FIGURE 8.1 THE PERSONNEL SYSTEM

PERSONNEL SYSTEM	FUNCTIONS
Hiring	• Application • Screening • Assessment • Interview • Decision
Induction	• Introduction to staff/team/department members • Overview of organizational history, structure, vision, culture, values • Review of contract • Review of school handbook/district policy manual • Job description—roles and responsibilities • Review of teaching schedule • Work health and safety information • Tour of building and teaching workstations • Review of key dates • Providing work tools (ID, keys, phone, etc.)
Training	• The assignment of a mentor • Orientation sessions with team/department/division leaders • Orientation to teacher evaluation plan
Supervision	• Staffing • Curriculum development • Instructional supervision (teacher evaluation) • Operation and application of technology systems • Accomplishment of school improvement goals

Each year, usually during the month of March, school districts determine their staffing needs. From that month on, the personnel function becomes a priority in all main offices. AGJs are adept at fully staffing their schools with qualified candidates before the first school bell rings in the fall; every classroom is staffed by teachers qualified to teach a particular grade level, a particular subject, or a particular specialty.

AGJs are also efficient with the remaining functions of a school's personnel system. Once the hiring and induction personnel functions have been completed, the remaining developmental functions—training and supervision—are often handed off to other administrative personnel or lead teachers. Similar to the other personnel functions, the training and supervision of new staff follow district and school protocols that prescribe the managerial instruments and timelines for each personnel function. AGJs, along with their managerial team members, efficiently and fully document the completion of all training and supervision functions within prescribed timelines.

These institutional goals and practices of main office personnel systems are poorly designed to develop the dispositions, skills, orientation, and identities that inspire and motivate both staff and students. Administrators and teachers have come to terms with personnel systems that provide them with tools and processes to simplify the task of developing the talent in their buildings. Administrators focused solely on meeting contractual timelines for the prescribed number of observations, conferences, and paperwork miss the opportunity to develop the individual talents of teachers. Teachers focused solely on teaching in accordance with district performance criteria and the particular preferences of their administrative supervisors miss the opportunity to expand their emotional and intellectual commitment to teaching repertoires.

THE HOUSE OF PERFORMANCE CARDS

The institutional attempt to impose rational methods on behaviors, processes, and practices that are fundamentally ambiguous creates behaviors, processes, and practices that are built on an institutional house of cards. Removing any one of these institutional cards would result in the collapse of the entire system. The cards include the following:

- **Card #1:** The importance of teacher evaluation criteria
- **Card #2:** The meaning of teacher evaluation criteria
- **Card #3:** The narrative assessment of a teacher evaluation
- **Card #4:** The interchangeable observer role
- **Card #5:** The meaning of feedback
- **Card #6:** The correction of shortcomings

The self-authoring stance of SSLs allows them to recognize how each card in the personnel process can be left in place but repurposed into a foundation for building talented teaching.

Card #1: Use Criteria Patterns to Enhance Deep Learning

At the center of all school personnel systems are teacher evaluation instruments listing teaching behaviors that will be observed and documented. When questioned about the importance of each criterion, administrators provide the following responses:

- "They are all important."

- "I need to see all criteria when I observe your classroom."

- "Some are more important than others, but they all need to be present."

These responses overlook how the criteria can work together to author a particular model of teaching that will achieve the educational goals and values listed in school mission statements. When SSLs work with teachers, the substance of their interaction is not about the presence or absence of criteria; for example, does the teacher state instructional objective at the beginning of class? When SSLs work with teachers, they discuss how a pattern of criteria can enhance deep learning outcomes; for example, how did the teacher develop sustained exchanges between themselves and their students to deepen understanding of a specific concept or goal?

Card #2: Use Teaching Behaviors to Enhance Deep Learning

School districts have adopted packaged teacher evaluation frameworks complete with pages of criteria for effective teaching, rubrics to assess levels of performance, and, in some frameworks, aggregate scores that equate to a rating on a district performance scale. All these managerial performance tools are based on behavioral categories such as classroom management, knowledge of subject matter, communication with students, and knowledge of students. These concepts are ambiguous at best and, at worst, highly subjective. Examples of these assessments include the following:

- The classroom culture is a cognitively busy place.

- Virtually all students are intellectually engaged in challenging content.

- Teacher displays extensive knowledge of the important concepts in the discipline.

- Teacher takes a leadership role with colleagues.

When SSLs work with teachers, the substance of their interaction is not about the meaning of various teaching criteria but about how *specific teaching behaviors* can enhance deep learning outcomes. Examples include the following:

- The lesson design, activity structures, and classroom organization are aimed at teams of students solving a real-world problem.

- Throughout the lesson, Mrs. X posed the following types of questions: factual, convergent, divergent, and evaluative.

- Classroom discussion evidenced student understanding of discussion ground rules, student understanding of the question under discussion, continuous student-to-student interchanges, and frequent summaries of positions of the contributors.

- All elements of cooperative learning—face-to-face interaction, individual accountability, group processing, and equal opportunity to participate— were present in the lesson design.

Card #3: Use the Narrative for Personal Reflection

In addition to the metrics imposed by district evaluation plans—rubrics, rating descriptors, and scores—the last page of the evaluation asks for a narrative assessment of the teacher's skills. However, teachers and administrators alike know that it is impossible to quantify the countless social, emotional, and intellectual variables that fly around during a classroom lesson. When SSLs work with teachers, the substance of their interaction is the teacher's personal reflection on which teaching behaviors resulted in deep learning and which teaching behaviors were less effective in achieving deep learning outcomes.

A postconference conducted by an SSL would replace the usual narrative evaluative comments with questions that invite a teacher to think about and reflect upon the lessons they have taught or are planning to teach. In a typical planning or postconference, an SSL would ask the following questions:

- "As you see the lesson unfolding, what will students be doing?"

- "As the lesson unfolds, what will you be doing first? Next? Last?"

- "As you reflect on the goals of the lesson, what can you say about your students' achievement of them?"

- "As you plan for future lessons, what ideas have you developed that might be carried forth to the next or other lessons?"

- "What will you see students doing or hear them saying that will indicate to you that your lesson is successful?"

Card #4: Use the Most Qualified Observer

The attraction of all packaged teacher evaluation plans is a framework that lists generic teaching behaviors that can be observed and evaluated by any administrator in the school. Problems arise when an administrator lacks the academic or pedagogical background in the lessons they are to observe. When SSLs work with teachers, the substance of their interaction centers on explicit understandings of the effective teaching of the subject they are observing. If an SSL is lacking that proper pedagogical background, they will seek out a qualified supervisor.

Card #5: Use Feedback to Enhance Performance

The most important component of any teacher evaluation plan is providing teachers with feedback on lessons that were observed, or on other aspects of their performance in the classroom. An underlying problem with the feedback function is the habit of supervisors to believe that a teacher's performance, whether superior or marginal, reflects who the teacher is—their drive, style, or effort. When an SSL works with a teacher, the substance of their interaction is not about *who* the teacher is but about aspects of the teacher's performance, such as the *what*, *why*, and *how* of the lessons observed. A postconference conducted by an SSL would replace evaluative comments regarding the teacher's style of instruction or personal subject matter interests with questions that invite teachers to think about the substance of the lesson that was observed. For example:

> "Ms. Larson, in the lesson I observed, the stated objective of the lesson was tracing the rise of the civil rights movement. In the course of the lesson, you referenced the construction of Three Rivers Stadium as a key symbol in the efforts to combat discriminatory hiring practices. For the remainder of the period, you went into great detail about how Three Rivers Stadium got its name and how it was constructed, which then led into the recounting of the development of the steel industry in the Midwest. With regard to the lesson I observed, what are your thoughts on the relationship between the stated objective of the class (tracing the rise of the civil rights movement) and the lesson content of the history of Three Rivers Stadium and the development of the steel industry in the Midwest?"

Card #6: Use Observations to Develop Strengths

The logic of most teacher evaluation instruments is based on the belief that improvement of performance comes from remedying shortcomings on a prescribed list of teaching criteria. As already described, the performance house of cards constructed by district HR departments is built on performance criteria that are vague, lack an educational purpose, are impossible to measure, and are deficits based. These performance cards make it impossible to judge the level of performance on any particular set of competencies listed in a district's teacher performance plans. When SSLs work with teachers, the substance of their interaction is helping them develop the instructional strengths they bring into the classroom. A postconference conducted by an SSL would replace evaluative comments regarding the absence of certain teaching criteria with questions that invite a teacher to think about how they could improve upon an instructional strength. For example:

> "Mr. Bernard, in the lesson I observed, you frequently referenced stories that bring history alive in your classroom. Your storytelling performance clearly resonates with your students. Based on comments and questions from students, however, it appeared they were having difficulty connecting some of the details of the story with the historical concept you were developing. Regarding the lesson I observed, what are your thoughts about how to make clearer connections between the details of the story you told and the historical concept you were developing?"

STRENGTHS-BASED PERFORMANCE

A core belief of SSLs is that talent plays an essential role in creating learning environments that can achieve the educational goals and values written into school mission statements. This core belief is founded on two principles of teaching and learning. First, that excellence in any profession is idiosyncratic. Every teacher brings into the classroom a unique and distinct set of skills. Second, the greatest advance in individual teacher performance comes from focusing on cultivating these unique and distinct skills, not from working on perceived deficits listed on a district's teacher evaluation plan.

A strengths-based performance system is designed to develop the individual talents of a teacher within an instructional methodology that would best achieve the agreed-upon goals and purposes of the subject being taught.

A strengths-based performance system is designed to develop the individual talents of a teacher within an instructional methodology that would best achieve the agreed-upon goals and purposes of the subject being taught. Instead of a performance plan focused on a teacher's execution of a list of criteria, a strengths-based plan focuses on how particular talents brought into the classroom will achieve the goals and purposes of the subject being taught. Resource 8.1 provides an example of an instructional framework a district could develop for a particular subject in its course offerings.

An instructional framework is not a list of teaching criteria but rather a conceptual framework for connecting the instructional principles that a faculty authors to best achieve an agreed-upon educational outcome. Although teachers may agree in theory with a particular instructional framework, the way that framework is implemented in any given classroom may be quite different. Resource 8.1, for example, outlines a constructivist instructional methodology. Teachers whose strengths are based on direct teaching methodologies would feel awkward working within a discovery instructional framework. To stand out, AGJs must pay attention to the gaps between differing teaching models and the individual teaching strengths of their faculties. They must expand their role beyond implementing the institutional particulars of an adopted instructional methodology: distribution of materials, training, data collection, and documentation.

To become an SSL, an AGJ must assume responsibility for employing their supervisory skills—listening, course-correcting, adjusting, coaching, pinpointing, and advising—to preserve individual teaching strengths and adapt those strengths to accommodate the principles of agreed-upon instructional methodology. Will all teachers become proficient in an agreed-upon instructional framework? Probably not. The aim of disciplined talent is not to develop clone-like classrooms but rather to bring diverse teaching dispositions and styles to a common set of educational goals and instructional principles.

Some teaching models are better than others in realizing an agreed-upon set of educational goals and instructional principles. The aim of disciplining talent is to help teachers develop a self-authoring mindset that consists of a purposeful commitment to adapting elements of a personalized teaching style to better achieve the goals and principles of an agreed-upon instructional framework. No matter what style of instruction a teacher prefers, there will always be a crack in that style for developing an alternative approach to curriculum organization and teaching methodologies. SSLs devote considerable time and preparation to assisting teachers with expanding and filling those cracks with elements of an agreed-upon instructional framework. A postconference conducted by an SSL would explore the cracks in a firmly held teaching methodology:

> Mr. Lynch, in observing your classes, there is no doubt that your direct teaching methods meet all the performance criteria related to the clarity of instruction. In addition, your methods clearly align well with our state testing instrument. Although we've had some disagreements over the merits of discovery learning formats, you've acknowledged that your classes should include more classroom discussions. I believe our conversations over the merits of direct teaching versus discovery learning have approached the differing philosophies from an *either/or* stance rather than a *both/and* integration. In this classroom observation, I noticed several instances in the lesson that offered fertile ground for a discussion format. In fact, in one instance a discussion was started, but you ran out of time to fully develop the discussion. If you're open to exploring the *both/and* option, I have several resources you might take a look at that illustrate discussion formats within a direct teaching model. You might also talk with Ms. Shah in your department. In her classes she is a master of the discussion format.

WHAT ABOUT JANE?

While SSLs establish no performance ceilings in their schools, they *do* establish performance floors—minimum performance standards that are fundamental to effective teaching. Among these performance standards would be knowledge of subject matter, management of student behavior, a plan for instruction, and treatment of students. Teachers walk onto the performance floor when they provide students with incorrect knowledge, when their classes are regularly out of control, when they present disorganized lessons, or when they are rude or abusive to students.

All schools have teachers walking on the performance floor, but most administrators avoid addressing this. The common excuse for this is the formidable legal complexities of dismissing a tenured teacher. Although the dismissal procedures in most states are not as daunting as administrators would lead you to believe, the process does draw an administrator into a time-consuming and unpleasant face-to-face process of documentation, conferencing, and remediation that ultimately can lead to a formal hearing.

Another excuse for administrators' avoidance of this issue is the belief that addressing a teacher's position on the floor will damage morale. The occupational structure of the profession provides teachers with little opportunity to advance in it (achievement) and little opportunity for status or recognition (power). Teachers are left only with ample opportunities to be liked by colleagues and students and to become comfortable with going along with whatever the rest of the group desires.

While administrators are given opportunities for achievement and power, they still have spent some years working within a culture of group belonging and collaboration. This underlying history is expressed in main offices that go out of their way to avoid personnel situations that are confrontational and judgmental. The fact remains that either choice—avoiding dealing with teachers who are on the performance floor or addressing the problem—will almost always result in faculty expressions of low morale, which is an issue that no administrator wants to wrestle with for long.

AGJs would admit to having a performance floor in their building and would assert that their administrative team promptly responds to all issues related to classroom performance. This response by AGJs, however, is merely a continuation of avoiding issues with the floor. AGJs use various managerial tools to transfer a struggling teacher into instructional venues that will cause the least amount of academic harm to students and get them out of any instructional situation where they would come into contact with the children of influential

> *SSLs are well aware of the managerial tools to work around their school's performance floor, but they believe these tools marginalize the value of talent and threaten the social, emotional, and intellectual development of their students.*

parents. The goal of this is to avoid the legal and cultural downsides of terminating a teacher while at the same time minimizing the academic effects of poor teacher performance. The vignette titled "Transferring Jane to a Different Department" illustrates how an AGJ might work around the fact that Jane is walking on the performance floor.

TRANSFERRING JANE TO A DIFFERENT DEPARTMENT
Charles Bookman (principal) to Jane Ferguson (teacher)

"Jane, I know our assistant principal, Ms. Jacobson, has expressed to you her concerns about your ability to control your classroom. Several students have been injured in lab situations that weren't monitored carefully. I've talked with Mr. Thomason, our union representative, about your situation. We agreed that a less demanding role for you in our school is in order. We're looking for a half-time supervisor in our media center as well as a supervisor for some open study hall periods for the coming school year. Mr. Thomason and I agreed that you would be a good fit for those positions. I know how much time and effort you have put into your program, but those same skills will serve us well in the media center and study hall supervision."

SSL TIP
Valuing Talent

SSLs are well aware of the managerial tools they can use to work around their school's performance floor, but they believe these tools marginalize the value of talent and threaten the social, emotional, and intellectual development of their students.

SSLs uphold the essential role talent plays in their school by replacing the performance floor with a performance standard for teaching (see Figure 8.2). SSLs may include various qualities of performance in the standard, but at a minimum it should include the following:

- the teacher knowing the *what*, *why*, and *how* of what they are talking about

- respect for diverse talents, abilities, and interests of students

- engagement of a child's social need to be known, emotional need to be interested, and intellectual need to understand the world around them

- professional need to reflect on practice

(Continued)

(Continued)

No matter what teaching style or model a teacher may prefer, what matters most to an SSL is that teachers in their school demonstrate a common understanding and commitment to an agreed-upon performance standard.

FIGURE 8.2   A PERFORMANCE STANDARD FOR TEACHING

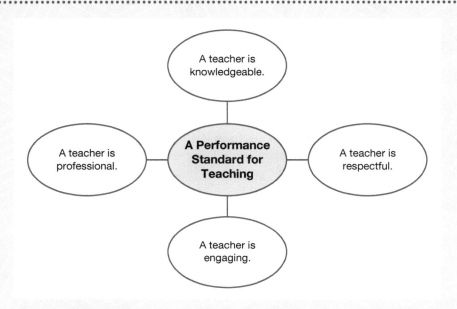

Of all the leadership attributes of SSLs, one that truly makes them stand out from their colleagues is their handling of teachers lodged on the performance floor. AGJs are managerial driven; SSLs are value driven. If talent is a strong value, then teachers falling below an agreed-upon performance standard cannot be managed around; they must be confronted. How that confrontation is played out depends upon the legislative rules, legal processes, contractual agreements, and personalities of the professionals involved in the process. The narrative titled "Jane Leaves the Science Department" illustrates how one SSL confronted the situation of Jane walking on the performance floor.

JANE LEAVES THE SCIENCE DEPARTMENT
Aaron Kaplan (principal) to Jane Ferguson (teacher)

"Jane, I know our assistant principal, Ms. Jacobson, has expressed to you her concerns about your ability to control your classroom. Several students have been injured in lab situations that weren't monitored carefully. In past performance reviews, Ms. Jacobson has noted your failure to closely monitor student behavior in these situations. Last year we brought in a consulting teacher to assist you with developing a behavioral plan for your classes and instituted weekly meetings with your department chairperson regarding the implementation of that plan. Based on the performance reviews submitted to me by Ms. Jacobson and the chair, Mr. Walsh, I became involved in the remediation process in January. Since January I have observed your classroom performance twelve times and used the coding method I discussed with you to document off-task behavior. As you can see from my summative evaluation of your performance, students in your class spent the majority of time engaged in what the coding system defines as off-task behavior: 'self-distraction,' 'peer distraction,' 'supply distractions,' 'environmental distractions,' and others. Based on these observation reports, I am rating your performance as unsatisfactory. I've scheduled a meeting with you next week to discuss the process for terminating your employment in this district. Others who will attend this meeting include your union representative, Mr. Thomason; our board attorney; and the teachers' association attorney."

A value in any organization emerges from what leaders act upon. For SSLs, the development of talent in the classroom is a core value. SSLs enact that value by adhering to the following three principles of talent development: First, provide teachers with the time, materials, and expertise to continually develop their individual instructional strengths. Second, provide teachers with the time, materials, and expertise to adapt their strengths to an agreed-upon instructional framework. Third, hold teachers accountable for meeting an agreed-upon standard of performance. Talent—disciplined talent—in schools led by SSLs is not a negotiable tool or a managerial tool but rather an essential quality to make the schools stand out.

1. What beliefs about the nature and practice of teaching guide your decisions regarding the employment and supervision of teachers in your building?

2. Based on your experience in supervising teachers, what would be your definition of a *talented* teacher?

3. What are the strengths and weaknesses of the teacher performance instrument your district has adopted?

4. Would you characterize your current teacher performance plan as a strengths-based or deficits-based instrument? Specifically, what components of the plan are based on strengths or which are based on deficits?

5. What do you find to be the most difficult parts of your postconferences with teachers?

6. How has your district defined weak teaching performance? How has your school addressed weak teaching performance?

RESOURCES

PRINCIPLE	DESCRIPTOR
Goals and purposes	The knowledge and skills developed in this subject will contribute to the following educational aims: • the awareness of complexity • the disposition to see other perspectives • the awareness of the limitations of knowledge • sensitivity to different contexts • the ability to reason analytically and critically • the ability to acquire knowledge and skills and make productive use of them
Pedagogy	The school program will ask teachers to include in their lessons the following elements of the effective teaching of their discipline: • elicit students' ideas/experiences in relation to key concepts • give students frequent opportunities to engage in complex, meaningful, and problem-based activities • provide students with a variety of information resources • allow students to work collaboratively and give them support to engage in task-oriented dialogue with one another • make their own thinking explicit to students and encourage them to do the same • routinely ask students to apply knowledge in diverse and authentic contexts, explain ideas, interpret texts, predict phenomena, and construct arguments based on evidence rather than recite predetermined "right" answers • employ a variety of assessment strategies to understand how students' ideas are evolving
Curriculum	The school program will follow these principles of curriculum: • Course offerings will focus on essential ideas, concepts, themes, and methods. • Course offerings will focus on the connection between these ideas, concepts, themes, methods, and applications. • Course offerings must include situations, applications, and contemporary problems that would demonstrate their usefulness.
Assessment	The school will develop multiple formative and summative assessment instruments to evaluate the achievement of the goals of the course offering and alignment with the district's instructional framework.
Training regime	The district will be responsible for designing and implementing a training program that addresses the effective application of the agreed-upon instructional framework (see Resource 8.2).

RESOURCE 8.2   A DISTRICT'S TEACHER TRAINING PROGRAM

COMPONENT	WHAT TEACHERS ARE ASKED TO DO
Goals and purposes	Identify gaps between agreed-upon goals/purposes and actual student performance.
Theories and practices	Identify a model of teaching that would best close the gaps between goals/purposes and actual student performance.
Model	Observe expert performance of an agreed-upon model of teaching.
Adapt	Under the supervision of a mentor/consultant, identify elements of a model of teaching that conform to personal teaching depositions and styles.
Coach	Participate in ongoing conversations with mentor/consultant on gaps between the intentions of an agreed-upon model of teaching and actual performance of those methods in classrooms.
Practice	Under the supervision of a mentor/consultant, continue to employ feedback from coaching sessions to close gaps between the intentions of an agreed-upon model of teaching and actual performance of those methods in classrooms.
Author	Construct pedagogical approaches and plans of action that agree with a school's instructional framework, the social context of the school, and preexisting experiences of teachers.
Standardize	Normalize teaching methods that make sense to teachers, are working for teachers, and accurately reflect the application of an agreed-upon model of teaching.

CHAPTER 9

....

CONTROLLING NARRATIVES

*I*n this chapter I discuss the power of different vocabularies and interpretative frameworks that control how school communities make sense of how schools work and how they ought to work. The conversation excerpts here illustrate the goals, values, and practices expressed by members of the school community. Each community "controls" the narrative in ways that support its personal vision of schooling. The first four narratives are personal expressions of the what and how of schooling. The final narrative finds a principal questioning the why of schooling.

CENTRAL OFFICE NARRATIVE
Laura Edwards (superintendent) and Marvin Olson (principal)

Superintendent Edwards:	Marvin, thanks for coming over on such short notice. I know this is a busy time for you. As you know from our strategic planning retreat, the board feels that our district isn't getting enough publicity.
Principal Olson:	Yes, several board members did ask me about our PR process at the retreat.
Superintendent Edwards:	The board is concerned that the upcoming referendum will be a stretch for our community unless we can demonstrate to them what an excellent school system we have. One of the board members suggested that winning a BlueRibbon award of excellence would garner us a lot of publicity and give all of us positive talking points next year. Of course, I thought of your school immediately. Your school's rise in test scores, your alternative drop-out program, Ms. Daniels becoming Teacher of the Year, and a state championship in softball would make you a shoo-in for the award.

(Continued)

(Continued)

Principal Olson:	Thanks for thinking of our school for this. I'm familiar with the Blue Ribbon award. Your predecessor asked me to apply several years ago. I did read the application and talked with winners in other districts, but I told Dr. Jorgensen that with all the issues I was dealing with at my school, I had no time to complete the application process.
Superintendent Edwards:	Marvin, we desperately need those referendum monies. Our buildings are in poor condition, and without more funding we're going to have to make drastic staff reductions next year. I believe winning that award would put us in the driver's seat. I do understand your position, however, and the board is willing to provide you with whatever help you need to complete the application. I've already talked to a consultant who has a lot of experience with the Blue Ribbon process, and I'll send over all the secretarial help you need.
Principal Olson:	Dr. Edwards, I appreciate your comments about my school, and I do understand the importance of passing that referendum next year. I have a few Saturdays with little going on at school. With that help, I believe we can complete the application.

BUILDING NARRATIVE
Terri Jacobson (assistant principal) and Larry Elmore (principal)

Asst. Principal Jacobson:	Larry, did you read the revised state guidelines for submission of our school improvement plan?
Principal Elmore:	I did read them, but they are still sending me to an all-day meeting at the county office to review each section of the plan.
Asst. Principal Jacobson:	All day?
Principal Elmore:	Yes. Right in the middle of budget meetings and dealing with that fight at the football game.
Asst. Principal Jacobson:	Doesn't Mary Anne in data processing pretty much handle the numbers on the plan?
Principal Elmore:	Yes, she is a lifesaver. I don't know what half of those numbers mean, but at least they fill in the blank boxes. Don, our cirriculum director, handles the remainder of the plan. He is really into those key performance indicators.
Asst. Principal Jacobson:	What about the fight?

Principal Elmore:	Our police liaison officer is handling that. At this point it appears to be just a fight over some confrontation at Winslow Park. No weapons or gangs seem to be involved.
Asst. Principal Jacobson:	What I am worried about are these budget cuts. Dave, the business manager, is back to his across-the-board cuts again. Every year we go through the same discussion. He can't understand that each department has different needs. A 20 percent cut to science is not the same thing as a 20 percent cut to English. And I will lose it if he asks me one more time about the cost of fetal pigs.
Principal Elmore:	I need to get to lunch supervision.
Asst. Principal Jacobson:	Oh, did Dr. Williams move up the date for our final observation write-ups?
Principal Elmore:	Yes, by a whole month. I haven't been in one class yet. How about you?
Asst. Principal Jacobson:	I have a couple of write-ups, but next week you won't see me. I will be in classrooms all day. I'm meeting briefly with the teachers after class and counting that as a postconference. It saves a lot of time.
Principal Elmore:	I'm going to start doing that if I ever get into a class. Can't be today. I'm going to the police station to see about that fight.

TEACHER NARRATIVE
Teacher #1 (Aisha) and Teacher #2 (Cynthia)

Teacher #1:	Cynthia, it's just a typical opening day, without the great donuts this year.
Teacher #2:	Yes, no donuts, but, as always, we have a new program, a new administrator, and of course we continue to 'strive for excellence.'
T1:	What does a data management specialist do?
T2:	I have no idea, but he's making a presentation this afternoon.
T1:	Why can't we just get into our classrooms? Mine is a mess from this summer's construction. I have to unpack my boxes of materials. There is just so much to do.
T2:	Me too. At least you have your old classroom. They moved me down the hall to Room 201.
T1:	How are you going to fit thirty kids into Room 201? It's the size of a large closet!

PARENT NARRATIVE

Parent #1 and Parent #2 (Judy)

Parent #1: Judy, my son was accepted into the gifted and talented program at Whittier!

Parent #2: Terrific! My daughter was in that program last year. They pile on the homework, but for the first time, I saw her being challenged.

P1: I'm really pleased we moved into this district. They have so many programs and extracurricular activities.

P2: Yes, we are too. My son plays two sports in high school and is in the band. He's enrolled in two AP courses. He wanted to get into a third one, but we thought it might be a little bit too much. Would you be interested in coming with Fred and me to the opening of the new swimming complex?

P1: Yes, we would. I saw pictures of it in the district newsletter. Really impressive that we could have an Olympic-level facility in our community.

P2: My daughter is a swimmer. We're giving her lessons. She's a couple of years away from high school, but we can't wait for her to see the facility.

P1: Too bad Mr. Katz is retiring. He was a great principal. He knew the names of all his students, attended all the games, and really helped me get my daughter out of Mrs. James's class last year.

P2: Honestly, I don't know why they keep her on.

P1: Well, you know unions have made it impossible to remove a bad teacher.

P2: Yeah, I guess they have. Oh, you might think about attending the school board meeting next month. They're proposing a new math curriculum.

P1: Not the one they are using over at Glenview? The kids over there don't even know the times table.

P2: That's the one.

P1: Kenji and I will be there.

STUDENT NARRATIVE

Student #1 (Emerson) and Student #2 (Vince)

Student #1: Vince, you want to cut fifth period and get some decent food at McDonald's?

Student #2: No, I'm skipping lunch. I have to go to the media center and finish up Glassman's last learning packet.

S1: Why don't you just copy mine? You know he never really reads them. He just marks ten points and hands out the next packet.

S2:	I'd rather do those packets than listen to him talking about the battles of the Civil War for the entire period.
S1:	Yeah, last week I thought we'd never get off that mountain. Where was it?
S2:	Gettysburg.
S1:	Who cares who got flanked or what general got shot?
S2:	That's why I do those packets. I need those points to make up for my Ds and Cs on those mind game tests.
S1:	That last one was a real gem. Any other normal teacher writes a straight multiple-choice question. Not Mr. Glassman. We have to select if it is an A only, B only, or both A and B. Come on Glassman, get in the game!
S2:	And those essays. 'Was Grant an overrated general?' He won the war, didn't he?
S1:	Then he tells us that he is teaching critical thinking. What a joke. Remember when Ava questioned him about the removal of those Confederate statues? First time I saw the man speechless.
S2:	He never did answer the question. We had to move on to get ready for Friday's test. You know, I changed my mind. Let's go to McDonald's today.

SSL NARRATIVE

Dr. Levine (principal) and Dr. Chavez (consultant)

Principal Levine:	Dr. Chavez, I appreciate you seeing me on short notice. As I said over the phone, I'm not pleased with our bilingual program. At several conferences on the subject, your name came up numerous times as a leader in the field.
Dr. Chavez:	No problem, Dr. Levine. I'll make time for anyone looking to improve the experiences of ELL learners.
Principal Levine:	My concern is the number of students in our program who are dropping out.
Dr. Chavez:	While I would agree that the drop-out rate for ELL students is certainly a concern, you're asking the wrong question.
Principal Levine:	What should I be asking?

(Continued)

(Continued)

Dr. Chavez:	The question I would be asking is, how many of your ELL students are going to college?
Principal Levine:	Going to college? My goal is to get them a high school diploma."
Dr. Chavez:	Yes, certainly that's an admirable goal, but asking the college question gets to the heart of the problem
Principal Levine:	What's the problem?
Dr. Chavez:	The problem is that you have several ELL students in your bilingual program who have rich academic backgrounds. Instead of being placed in courses that match their academic backgrounds, they are being placed in basic skills classes. These students feel insulted and are bored in classes that don't reflect their cognitive understandings.
Principal Levine:	But these students speak little English. There is no way they could succeed in our upper-level academic classes.
Dr. Chavez:	Yes, there is a way for them to succeed in such classes.
Principal Levine:	You mean, place a bilingual aide in those classes.
Dr. Chavez:	No, that intervention hasn't worked well for those students.
Principal Levine:	What does?
Dr. Chavez:	You place them in native-language academic courses, taught by certified academic teachers who are native speakers.
Principal Levine:	Where do I find native-speaking certified teachers in those areas?
Dr. Chavez:	Oh, they're out there. I could help you recruit those candidates if you're interested. Before you answer, I know what you are thinking. Your board is going to have a difficult time employing native-speaking academic teachers for courses now taught in English.
Principal Levine:	Exactly. What my board members will say to me is that these ELL students need to learn to speak English. The best way to learn English is to be immersed in classes taught in English.
Dr. Chavez:	We have an awful lot of research that says these students, especially at their cognitive level, will learn how to speak English. They are enrolled in your bilingual program, which is the appropriate venue for learning a second language. In the meantime, however, they need to maintain and grow their academic vocabularies and concepts in upper-level academic courses. These are the vocabularies and concepts that will best prepare them for college entrance exams and allow them to submit transcripts reflecting completion of a college-bound curriculum.
Principal Levine:	Your recommendation would be a tough sell for our board.

Dr. Chavez:	Yes, I know. I'd be willing to help you put together a presentation for your board. Before you decide how you want to approach this problem, I recommend that you sit down and examine the transcripts of the students currently enrolled in your bilingual program. Ask your guidance counselors how these incoming ELL students are placed. I'm sure that you'll find that most of your ELL students have been incorrectly placed in lower-level course offerings. I'm also sure that if you question recent dropouts from your school, they'll confirm my view that they decided they were better off getting a job than spending time in courses that they took years ago and that were not preparing them for college.
Principal Levine:	Dr. Chavez, again, I appreciate your insights into our dropout problem. I'll sit down with members of our guidance department to discuss the issues you've brought up. Certainly you've offered me a very different perspective on the problem than the one I got from the literature I've read and comments from our guidance staff.

CONTROLLING NARRATIVES

Members of a school community have different ways of understanding how schools operate and how they *should* operate. Each of these narratives illustrates how these community members discuss their school experiences. They author their narrative using specific vocabularies and frameworks to control the presentation of information in order to shape public opinion or maintain a desired image or viewpoint. The controlling narrative authored by those in *central offices* projects the image of a school that is exceptional, attractive, and entertaining. The controlling narrative authored by those in *building offices* depicts safe, responsive, and efficient management of a school. The controlling narrative authored by those in *classrooms* portrays teachers as underresourced, unheard, and overwhelmed. The controlling narrative authored by *parents* gives the impression of order, rigor, and excellent facilities. The controlling narrative authored by *students* focuses on conforming to routines, rules, and systems. The controlling narrative authored by *SSLs* utilizes methods of inquiry that question, analyze, and experiment.

While narratives will change somewhat from community to community, the six narratives that introduce this chapter represent common expressions of how superintendents, principals, teachers, parents, students, and SSLs make sense of the daily experiences in their respective schools. Every day school administrators find themselves entering a maze of narratives that articulate different goals, values, and practices. Divergent narratives are the result of organizational structures that are designed around two opposing goals of schooling: the institutional goal to *control* and the educational goal to *empower* (see Figure 9.1).

FIGURE 9.1 OPPOSING NARRATIVES OF SCHOOLING

COMPONENT	INSTITUTIONAL NARRATIVE (Authoritarian)	EDUCATIONAL NARRATIVE (Empowering)
Goal	• Ensure compliance • Prescribe performance • Focus on safety, security, and structure	• Go beyond competence • Promote autonomy • Focus on commitment (a cause beyond self)
Characteristics	• External reinforcements • Employee compliance with limits of the organization • Restricted individual choice • Familiarity with (and obeisance of) norms and minimum expectations of organization • Lists	• Expanded choice and opportunities to decide • Expanded sources of feedback • Freedom to choose according to interests and curiosity
Reaction of school community member	• Resistance/oppositional behavior • Resentment towards controller • Feelings of powerlessness, dependency, and passivity	• Driven to be powerful, independent, and active • Committed to become an initiator
Vocabulary	• Must • Should • Ought to • Need to	• Can • Could • Consider • Might

AGJs reconcile these opposing goals by becoming fluent in the multiple narratives voiced in their school community. Sitting in a superintendent's office, AGJs speak the language of goals, strategic plans, mandates, and funding. Sitting in a principal's office, they speak the language of schedules, systems, operations, and budgets. Sitting in PTA meetings, AGJs speak of programs, awards, facilities, and events. Sitting in a student advisory group, they speak of achievement, honors, and responsibilities.

In each narrative AGJs will intersperse their particular narrative with the vocabularies of empowerment—autonomy, choice, innovation, diversity, flexibility, relevance, and personalization. When they leave these gatherings, however, they return to offices dominated by narratives grounded in the beliefs, values, and practices of a bureaucratic model of schooling that prizes simplicity over complexity, standardization over novelty, and stability over disruption.

Where SSLs depart from their colleagues is in authoring a narrative that includes the institutional realities of the schools they work in but at the same time advocates for organizational structures and pedagogical practices that live up to their school's educational goals and values.

Why does an SSL author, and then recite, a narrative that runs counter to the beliefs, values, and practices of the controlling narratives encircling their office? First, when administrators walk into a school, they can be assured that staff and faculty are viewing them through a lens created by the theories, ideas, and practices gathered in their lives and careers that helps them author a narrative that makes sense of their personal and professional lives. The substance of that narrative will control how a school community will interpret, support, and carry out school policies, procedures, and practices.

> *[SSLs author] a narrative that includes the institutional realities of the schools they work in but at the same time advocates for organizational structures and pedagogical practices that live up to their school's educational goals and values.*

Secondly, the normative theories, ideas, and practices that shape a particular narrative originate from the daily interactions between school community members over problematic situations in their school. That narrative will become the foundation for diagnosing the cause of a schoolwide problem and developing a solution to that problem. Figure 9.2 represents how differing narratives in a school could shape how teachers might think and talk about the four common problems of schooling.

FIGURE 9.2 APPLYING OPPOSING NARRATIVES TO SCHOOLWIDE PROBLEMS

PROBLEM OF SCHOOLING	INSTITUTIONAL NARRATIVE (Authoritarian)	EDUCATIONAL NARRATIVE (Empowering)
The problem of institutions	The organizational structures and policies of a school should be designed to develop habits of punctuality, responsibility, and dependability.	The organizational structures and policies of a school should be designed to disrupt inequalities and create opportunities for social change and justice.
The problem of pedagogy	Teaching and learning are the accumulation of facts and skills learned through processes of practice and feedback.	Teaching and learning should be organized to cultivate active exploration in the service of real-world tasks.
The problem of goals	Our mission is to prepare students for success in the working world.	Our mission is the full development of the private and public self of each student.
The problem of experience	Teachers should provide students with the knowledge and skills they will need for mastery of disciplinary learning.	Teachers should build on the natural interests and capacities of students.

> *SSLs acknowledge the power that controlling narratives have to distort the best intentions of a change initiative or a mission-driven goal. Before an SSL begins the implementation process, they first spend time critiquing the goals, beliefs, and practices of the narrative that is controlling the process.*

AGJs pay little attention to controlling narratives. They believe that whatever goals, beliefs, ideas, or practices they are promoting will prevail over existing narratives. SSLs acknowledge the power that controlling narratives have to distort the best intentions of a change initiative or a mission-driven goal. Before an SSL begins the implementation process, they first spend time critiquing the goals, beliefs, and practices of the narrative that is controlling the process. Several narratives promoting schoolwide programs are founded on faulty research and disputed goals and values. If a narrative runs counter to the goals and practices of a proposed change initiative, SSLs author, and then promote, an alternative narrative that supports the goals, beliefs, and practices of the desired change initiative. Multiple controlling narratives hinder the ability to live up to a school's mission statement. SSLs transform controlling narratives into empowering narratives.

SSL TIP

Changing the Narrative

In the sense I am using the term, a *controlling narrative* represents a piece in a large mosaic of theories, ideas, and practices that forms a worldview of how the world works, how schools work, and how children learn. An SSL shapes the direction of a controlling narrative by providing the resources and logistics to grow it in a certain instructional direction. They do this by honoring specific theories, ideas, and practices over others; they select those theories, ideas, and practices from a variety of disciplines that fit a particular instructional or organizational problem. Most importantly, SSLs strategically author narratives that challenge prevailing worldviews voiced in their building.

Resource 9.1 provides several examples of how an SSL-authored narrative might sound at a faculty meeting. Faculty meetings are rich environments containing all sorts of worldviews of how schools should work and how children should learn. Typically, bits and pieces of these worldviews appear near the end of a faculty meeting when certain teachers assume the role of gadfly, taking turns asking the principal questions that always begin with the phrase "Has anyone given thought to. . .?" What follows this introductory phrase is not really a question but an expression of the controlling narrative authored by faculty and composed of their perceptions and solutions to the problem.

AGJs deflect these faculty narratives with managerial solutions to the problem, such as adding personnel, implementing new rules, redesigning a system, or adding a new technology. SSLs, however, recognize faculty narratives as opportunities to author counternarratives that ask members of the school community to respect other points of view; to recognize that most schoolwide problems involve complex interactions between countless variables; to remove emotion, as much as possible, from purposeful methods of inquiry; and, most importantly, to provide participants with opportunities to "try on" other realities, predict possible futures, and experience different viewpoints.

A well-crafted narrative alone, however, will not change how a school community talks about policies, procedures, or schoolwide problems. School administrators must create a context for the narrative for it to take root. SSLs use every available opportunity—faculty memos, meeting agendas, board meetings, building meetings, public gatherings, and brief encounters in hallways and parking lots—to communicate and model the beliefs, ideas, and practices promoted by their controlling narrative. It is in these different venues where an assortment of managerial moves—materials purchased, personnel employed, curriculum adopted, classroom visitations, and time spent in teacher workspaces—demonstrate to teachers how the words in the narrative translate into building and classroom practices.

Throughout the process of presenting, negotiating, and implementing the contents of a narrative, SSLs assume many roles, such as managers, leaders, champions, and entrepreneurs. No matter what role best promotes the narrative, SSLs always remain true to the educational values and goals written into their school mission statements.

REFLECTIVE QUESTIONS

- What narratives in your district control the goals and practices in your school?

- Of the narratives that control the goals and practices in your school, which are the most helpful in pursuing mission-driven goals and which are the most harmful in pursuing mission-driven goals?

- In your current administrative role, what narratives have served as obstacles for pursuing mission-driven goals? How have you countered those narratives?

RESOURCES

RESOURCE 9.1 CHANGING THE NARRATIVE

SCHOOLWIDE PROBLEM	"HAS ANYONE GIVEN THOUGHT TO. . .?"	VALUED END OF SCHOOLING	HOW SSLs CHANGE THE NARRATIVE
Attendance	*A five-step attendance policy?* After five absences, no matter what the reason, students are dropped from class.	"Our school is committed to being respectful and responsive to the individual needs of our student body."	"As you know, we have been working for the last two years on curricular programs and support services designed to pull students into our school instead of policies and rules designed to push them out. The other consideration is that we have demographic groups in our district that would be adversely affected by policies that are in opposition to various cultural traditions."
Grading	*Instituting a weighted grade system?* Students in honors classes are rewarded for hard work and taking more difficult classes.	"Our school is committed to honoring the diverse abilities, interests, and goals of our student body."	"Let me begin by questioning the assumption that students in honors classes are working harder than students in basic tracks. If we are placing students appropriately, then all students in our school are being challenged and working hard in their classes. Secondly, what I see in curriculum meetings are proposals that seek to address the diverse talents and abilities of students who enter our building. I feel that if we begin valuing certain subjects over other subjects, we send the message that certain talents and abilities are more important than others."
Bilingual education	*Eliminating our bilingual program?* The most effective approach to improve the literacy skills of Spanish speakers is immersing students in English-only classes.	"Our school is committed to building an inclusive school environment that welcomes students of all backgrounds."	"I know many of you have questioned our ELL program, specifically the development of classes in our students' native language (Spanish). We spent considerable time this summer discussing this question with a university consultant and our bilingual staff. Our consultant and the research both support that teaching students in their native language produces superior literacy results over immersion programs. I should add that a core value in our school mission statement is that we maintain the cultural identity of the student populations we serve."

SCHOOLWIDE PROBLEM	"HAS ANYONE GIVEN THOUGHT TO. . .?"	VALUED END OF SCHOOLING	HOW SSLs CHANGE THE NARRATIVE
School violence	*Reducing school violence?* Increase the penalties for fighting and hiring more security guards.	"Our school is committed to providing a safe learning and working environment for students and staff."	"When I interviewed for the principal's position at Central High, it was clear to me that school safety was your number one priority. I was also aware that the faculty have been requesting stiffer penalties for fighting and the employment of more security guards. During this summer, the deans and I spoke with several security experts and also spent some time looking at where and when fights occurred last year. We learned that stiffer penalties and more guards are not effective deterrents for the kinds of violence you experienced last year. By far the most effective deterrent is for faculty and administrators to take control of what they term 'unowned' areas in the school. To put it simply, the more adults you have in hallways and bathrooms, the less violence you will see in these areas. For the last two months, our administrative team has experimented with different supervisory schedules and found that the theory works, and it works very well. I will meet with faculty representatives this week to develop a supervisory schedule that will make all the unowned areas in our building owned by faculty and administrators."

CHAPTER 10

....

CRACKS IN THE SYSTEM

*I*n this chapter I discuss the role that organizational systems play in the *implementation of change initiatives. The conversation excerpts here reveal the cracks in a school's organizational systems that provide opportunities to advance mission-driven goals and values.*

Assistant Superintendent for Curriculum and Instruction to Principals	"Beginning next school year, we will be replacing our current teacher evaluation system with a new performance document focused on clinical supervision. A key element of this supervisory model is a cognitive coaching structure that places an emphasis on a teacher's thinking behind their practices rather on the various performance metrics we have used in the past."
Department Chair to Principal	"Principal Foster, I know you're in the process of building the master schedule. Just an FYI that Ms. Chen, the physics teacher, doesn't do mornings."
Teacher to Colleague	"Lisa, I'm using the sample scenarios from our curriculum guide, but they just aren't working for me. I admit they create a lot of discussion, but I'm having trouble guiding that discussion towards accomplishing an instructional objective. I know we've had many training sessions on this problem, but right now, I'm just so frustrated."
Principal to Human Resources Director	"Lou, I read about the changes you're making to our employment protocols. My concern is that the resume specifications and interview questions appear to place little emphasis on participation in extracurricular activities. While I understand the importance of subject matter knowledge, I hope we maintain a vigorous extracurricular program."

THE UNRUFFLED CALM

For decades, state and national legislatures, governmental agencies, professional associations, consultants, governors, and presidents have promoted mandates and programs to transform how public schools educate our children and adolescents. To use Larry Cuban's hurricane metaphor, the proposed mandates and programs create "surface turbulent waters" in state departments and main offices, while in classrooms, a "fathom below the surface," there is "unruffled calm" (Cuban, 1984, p. 2).

The failure of decades of school reform initiatives to take hold in school classrooms is blamed both on school leaders' failure to exercise their proper role of instructional leader and on a teaching profession opposed to instructional and curricular changes that would disrupt comfortable teaching routines. In the case of school leaders, AGJs take the yearly arrival of hurricane waters in stride. They quiet the turbulence of new teaching methodologies and innovative curricular initiatives by focusing on the tasks and functions—the *form*—of implementation.

> *The failure of decades of school reform initiatives to take hold in school classrooms is blamed both on school leaders' failure to exercise their proper role of instructional leader and on a teaching profession opposed to instructional and curricular changes that would disrupt comfortable teaching routines.*

The outcome of this implementation process for *central offices and governmental agencies* is documentation of compliance with the managerial functions associated with change initiatives: telling, allocating, training, and documenting. The outcome of this implementation process for *school classrooms* is surface representations of theories and practices that were intended to ruffle calm teaching routines. For decades, reform initiatives promising to transform outdated schooling models have fallen victim to the bargain struck between main offices satisfied with compliance and classrooms satisfied with calm waters.

> *While the focus of all school reform initiatives is on processes to assist teachers with repurposing how they think about and practice teaching, what is missing from these initiatives is repurposing the systems designed to achieve institutional goals.*

AIMS → GOALS → FUNCTIONS

SSLs avoid abstract critiques of school reform failure by focusing on the practicalities of implementing the *substance* of a change initiative. SSLs have witnessed firsthand how the managerial tools of implementation produce a reform experience that lacks coherence, substance, and collective sensemaking. While the focus of all school reform initiatives is on processes to assist teachers with repurposing how they think about and practice teaching, what is missing from these initiatives is repurposing the *systems* designed to achieve institutional goals. SSLs view the implementation process as both the repurposing of teacher thinking and the repurposing of the systems that support that thinking.

SSL TIP

Exploiting Cracks in the System

AGJs excel at developing and executing systems. The systems that consume the calendars of AGJs all involve managerial functions or tasks. From budgets to buses, AGJs spend their days fine-tuning systems that have well-defined goals, established methods, and prescribed outcomes. Even when an instructional system comes into play, they employ managerial tools to implement educational ends: Curriculum development converts to curriculum alignment; mandated teaching models convert to observation checklists; staff development converts to training sessions; state testing programs convert to test preparation courses.

SSLs grasp the power of systems to repurpose and redesign the aims and functions of a change initiative. The systems that draw the attention of SSLs all exercise some influence over instructional tasks and functions (see Resource 10.1). When mandated or innovative approaches to teaching enter their office, they initiate a process consisting of roughly three phases, as shown in Figure 10.1.

FIGURE 10.1

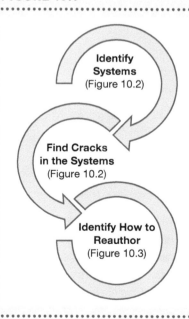

Identify
Systems
(Figure 10.2)

Find Cracks
in the Systems
(Figure 10.2)

Identify How to
Reauthor
(Figure 10.3)

PHASE I:
Identify the organizational systems that directly control the change initiative (see Figure 10.2).

PHASE II:
Find the components (cracks) in those systems that can be adapted to the aims and goals of the change initiative (see Figure 10.2).

PHASE III:
Identify how the components of the systems should be "reauthored" to enact the aims and goals of the change (see Figure 10.3).

(Continued)

(Continued)

If, for example, a district was adopting a proposed new teaching model, an SSL would first identify those systems with the most influence over the enactment of the aims and practices of the new teaching model (Phase I). They may determine that the level of complexity of the new teaching model requires a level of content background beyond the current training and backgrounds of their staff. In that case, employing teachers with similar theoretical and practical understandings would be the desirable strategy (Phase II). The remaining move is adjusting the functions of the system—standards, inputs, tasks, sequences, feedback—to achieve the reauthoring of that system (Phase III).

FIGURE 10.2   PHASES I AND II: IDENTIFYING SYSTEMS AND FINDING CRACKS

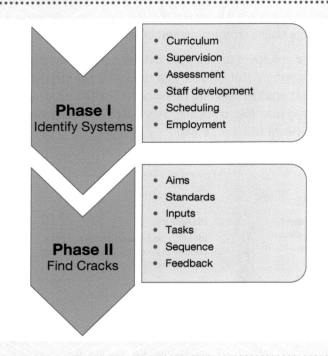

Reauthoring the employment system (as seen in Figure 10.3) will not change deeply held beliefs and practices about teaching and learning. With this reality in mind, SSLs must reauthor multiple systems so that teachers have little philosophical or instructional room to resist (in subtle or not-so-subtle ways). In the case of enacting a new teaching model, along with reauthoring the employment system an SSL may reauthor the staff development system to deepen understandings of subject matter content, reauthor the curricular system to incorporate activity structures compatible with new pedagogical practices, and/or reauthor the scheduling system to accommodate space and time configurations compatible with new pedagogical practices.

FIGURE 10.3 PHASE III: REAUTHORING A CRACK IN THE EMPLOYMENT SYSTEM

Aims

- How do we employ teachers with the knowledge base and dispositions that align with the agreed-upon subject matter configurations?

Standards: What areas will reflect standards of performance to achieve these aims?

- Grades
- Observations
- Examination of candidate's artifacts
- Interview
- Teaching demonstration

Inputs: What resources will be required to meet these aims?

- Processes
- Tools
- Personnel
- Materials
- Location
- Budget

Tasks

- Processes
- Routines
- Methods

Sequence: What order of functions will meet these aims?

- Stages
- Phases
- Steps

Feedback: Why is the system meeting/not meeting these aims?

- Problem
- Study
- Plan
- Act

(Continued)

(Continued)

Unfortunately, reauthoring one crack in one system is not sufficient to change how teachers think about, talk about, and practice new teaching models. Most new instructional models call for changing a teaching *culture*. Doing that requires reauthoring and redesigning the goals and functions of multiple systems that would affect the new model (see Resource 10.1).

In principle, reauthoring the cracks in the system is an effective strategy to shift a school culture. SSLs, however, are realists. They recognize that no matter how many systems they reauthor, or to what degree, they will be left with staff whose philosophical beliefs, teaching experiences, and work history engender different degrees of resistance to practicing the substance of a change initiative.

However, the aim of changing multiple systems is not to change individual minds. Reauthoring the cracks in multiple systems is designed to change an instructional culture. No matter how uncomfortable new theories or practices may be for a staff, they will be conducted within the vocabularies, the processes, and the activity structures of systems that are now designed to accommodate and enact the *substance* of newly adopted theories, ideas, and practices.

> *Systems instill goals, rituals, and routines. Over time, these goals, rituals, and routines author a new norm of teaching that will shift the thinking of some faculty and bring about gradations of compliance with others.*

Systems instill goals, rituals, and routines. Over time, these goals, rituals, and routines author a new norm of teaching that will shift the thinking of some faculty and bring about gradations of compliance with others. What matters to SSLs is that the intellectual and organizational frameworks to support the theories, ideas, and practices of a change initiative have been firmly positioned to detect and address deviance from a new norm of teaching and learning.

REFLECTIVE QUESTIONS

1. What systems in your school act as obstacles to achieving mission-driven goals and values? Which parts of these systems create the barriers?

2. In thinking about the systems in your building that directly control classroom teaching, what cracks, in your view, could be exploited to better repurpose the *how* and *what* of teaching?

3. What managerial steps would you implement to repurpose a system to better accommodate changes in teaching methodologies?

RESOURCES

RESOURCE 10.1   REAUTHORING TEACHING SYSTEMS

TEACHING SYSTEM	INSTITUTIONAL-DRIVEN PURPOSES (The *Why*)		MISSION-DRIVEN PURPOSES (The *Why*)	
	GOALS (The *What*)	FUNCTIONS (The *How*)	GOALS (The *What*)	FUNCTIONS (The *How*)
Supervision	To change classroom instruction by making teachers aware of gaps between classroom practices and performance standards	• Confront • Counsel	To change classroom instruction through clarification of teacher thinking	• Educate • Sponsor • Coach
Employment system	To employ teachers with appropriate certification and to fill extracurricular positions	• Evaluation of certifications/ credentials • Review of candidate's background in activities and/or athletics • Interview	To employ teachers with the knowledge base and dispositions to align with school's agreed-upon pedagogical principles and practices	• University training and grades • Observation(s) • Examination of candidate's artifacts • Interview • Teaching demonstration
Scheduling system	To construct a master schedule that complies with teacher preferences for grade and subject levels	• Teacher preference (subject-grade level/time of day) • Teacher experience • Teacher extracurricular duties	To construct a master schedule that optimizes teacher talents and enhances agreed-upon subject matter configurations	• Student preference (subject/ elective) • Student ability • Curriculum configuration (team teaching) • Teacher knowledge base
Staff development system	To design training that complies with mandated program goals and contemporary models of teaching	• Tell • Allocate • Inspect • Rectify	To design training that recognizes that adults learn best in an environment of trust and appreciation of differences	• Educate • Model • Coach • Author

CHAPTER 11

....

TOOLS

*I*n *this chapter I discuss how SSLs repurpose the goals and practices of established managerial tools to advance mission-driven goals and values. Five common managerial tools—budgets, personnel, teams, meetings, and master schedules—can be wielded in ways that either advance or hinder achieving the educational mission of schooling. The conversation excerpts here provide examples of these tools in action.*

Business Manager to Principal **(Budgets)**	"Principal Smith, the reduction in state revenues means we must take a hard look at our staffing allocations."
Principal to Assistant Principal **(Personnel)**	"Ben, based on the conversations we've had about the construction of the master schedule, I sense you're struggling with the mechanics of that job. I understand that the master schedule falls under your job description, but I've never looked upon job descriptions as set in stone. In looking over your resume, I see you have an extensive background in administering special education programs. Right now we're experiencing problems in our program, particularly with the handling of rules and regulations related to IDEA (Individuals With Disabilities Education Act). I'd appreciate it if you would team up with your co-assistant principal, Lisa, to address the challenges we are facing and reorganize the department in line with the changes you implemented at your former school. Beth, the data processing manager, and I will take care of the master schedule."
Team Member to Team Leader **(Teams)**	"Carolyn, you're supposed to be our team leader for implementing the Japanese lesson study protocol. What's happening with that? We haven't even discussed it because we've spent our last three meetings completing the state's school improvement forms."

(Continued)

(Continued)

Principal to Department Members (Meetings)	"Several months ago I met with Dr. Cortez, the bilingual coordinator from District 83, to discuss our high Latino dropout rates. I've invited him to our next meeting to share his recommendations to address the problem, some of which I found run counter to the current design of our program."
Principal to Athletic Director (Master Schedule)	"Bill, I understand why you requested the release of all your coaches from seventh period. I realize that a lot goes into preparing practice sessions. However, releasing that many personnel from teaching seventh period would limit student course requests. I'll take another look at the numbers, but as it stands now, I'll stick to my goal of honoring as many student requests as I can with the staff I have."

THE *HOW* AND *WHAT* OF MAIN OFFICES

The first part of this book (Chapter 1 through Chapter 10) described the different mindsets and practices of AGJs and SSLs. The essential distinction between these types of administrators is how they address the *why* of schooling. AGJs assume that the *why* of a change initiative is embedded in the *what* and *how* of implementation. SSLs, on the other hand, believe that the *why* of a change initiative must be clearly articulated and promoted. At this juncture in the book, I may have given the impression that as long as the *why* of a change initiative is understood, the *what* and *how* of that initiative will align with that *why*.

In Chapter 10 I explained how the *what* and *how* of systems will ultimately affect the enactment of the *why* of a change initiative. The same is true of the *what* and *how* of the managerial tools at hand. They will determine the *why* for carrying out a proposed change initiative. The use of the following five managerial tools lodged in school offices—budgets, personnel, teams, meetings, and a master schedule—will determine the level of enactment of any proposed change initiative.

Budgets

Every year central office administrators send each school a draft of the proposed budget for the coming school year. The budget proposal is developed by the finance manager, whose vocabularies, goals, values, and practices are often poorly aligned with the vocabularies, goals, and values of the schools they manage (see Resource 11.1).

In budget meetings, AGJs accept, with little question, the bottom-line narrative proposed by these district-level administrators. There will be some minor changes to the budget with the movement of monies to and from different line items, but rarely, if ever, will the total monies proposed be increased or educational priorities reestablished.

In these same meetings, SSLs will offer a counternarrative to proposed line-item allocations (see Resource 11.2). This *value-added* narrative offers educational rationales for reauthoring budgetary line items. By broaching the value-added narrative in the budgetary meeting, SSLs create an opportunity to convince district representatives to add monies to the proposed budget or to move around significant amounts of monies in various line items to achieve an agreed-upon educational goal. Although the value-added narrative may result in the marginalization of other educational goals and values, it provides SSLs with a tool to establish their authority over budgetary allocations and, more importantly, to direct monies into projects and programs that best represent agreed-upon mission-driven goals and values.

> *By broaching the value-added narrative in the budgetary meeting, SSLs create an opportunity to convince district representatives to add monies to the proposed budget or to move around significant amounts of monies in various line items to achieve an agreed-upon educational goal.*

Personnel

The optimum deployment and development of administrators, staff, and teachers are essential to quality stand-alone schools. Although all administrators would admit to the critical role that quality personnel play in their schools, AGJs and SSLs approach the personnel function with different philosophies and different managerial strategies.

AGJs' conception of human resource management begins with a model where administrators, staff, and teachers are assigned to specific roles that consist of lists of functions and tasks that are routinely performed by the personnel in those roles. The performance of these functions, tasks, and routines is controlled by a list of competencies whose mastery will determine the level of implementation. Any shortcomings in the implementation process are blamed on the failure of personnel to master a particular set of competencies. This personnel management model is founded on three administrative beliefs about the relationship between assigned job duties and individual performance (see Figure 11.1).

FIGURE 11.1   AGJS' PERSONNEL MANAGEMENT MODEL

PRINCIPLE	APPLICATION
Competencies are observable and measurable.	Fit the person's performance to prescribed competencies.
Those in each role possess a standard set of skills.	Fit the person's skills to the assigned role.
Improvement of performance comes from feedback.	Fit the person's learning to performance gaps.

SSLs have an entirely different set of beliefs about managing personnel in their buildings. First, they believe that competencies are impossible to observe or measure. Take critical thinking: Is it reflection in action, interpretation, or categorical thinking? Even if we could agree upon a definition, how would you measure the *level* of critical thinking, or explain to an administrator, staff, or teacher sitting in your office how critical thought relates to the implementation of functions, tasks, or routines?

Second, there is no standard set of skills. Each role in a school is composed of a set of knowledge, skills, and depositions unique to that role. Some roles lend themselves to applying technocratic skills to solving systems problems; others rely on academic skills to apply theories, philosophies, and concepts to real-world classroom problems; and still others call upon counseling skills to resolve conflicts between individual social, emotional, and intellectual behaviors.

Lastly, people get better at a job by improving on their strengths, not by remediating their weaknesses. No matter how conscientious an administrator, teacher, or staff member may be, improving a perceived weakness can be challenging. The underlying cause—whether intellectual, social, or emotional—often lies beyond the reach of typical remediation efforts. On the other hand, an administrator, teacher, or staff member can make great strides in enhancing and perfecting their strengths.

Based on this set of beliefs, SSLs author a strengths-based personnel management model (see Figure 11.2) that values

- solving problems over hitting a short-term metric,
- diverse viewpoints over perfunctory agreements,
- individual uniqueness over conformity, and
- excellence over compliance.

Although a strengths-based personnel management model requires the continual assessment and adjustment of personnel functions, tasks, and routines, this model provides SSLs with a tool that generates a managerial environment that is empowering, creative, and fulfilling.

FIGURE 11.2 SSLS' PERSONNEL MANAGEMENT MODEL

PRINCIPLE	APPLICATION
Outcomes are observable and measurable.	Tailor the *outcome* to the person's strengths.
Those in each role possess a unique set of abilities and talents.	Tailor the *job* to the person's strengths.
Improvement of performance comes from enhancing strengths.	Tailor *learning* to the person's strengths.

The fundamental difference between the two personnel models is how leaders view the relationship between job functions and employee skills. AGJs assume that staff have mastered basic skills to perform assigned office tasks and functions. When gaps appear in the performance of job functions and tasks, AGJs proceed to remediate deficiencies in a staff's skill set. The excerpt at the start of the chapter between a principal and his struggling assistant principal illustrates how SSLs would handle managerial mismatches. SSLs assume that staff enter their offices with a unique set of skills and dispositions. All tasks and functions assigned in SSL offices are tailored to optimize the unique skills and dispositions of staff. If gaps in performance arise, SSLs redesign the task or function or look to other skill sets in the office that would better perform the task or function. The exception to a strengths-based model are personnel that fail to respond to repeated interventions and coaching. For example, in the "What About Jane?" section in Chapter 8, an SSL departed from their AGJ colleague's popular decision to reassign teacher Jane Ferguson to the media center and instead made the unpopular decision to let Jane go. Figure 11.3 compares how AGJs and SSLs enact their understandings of managing personnel who report to them.

FIGURE 11.3   DEFICITS-BASED AND STRENGTHS-BASED PERSONNEL MODELS

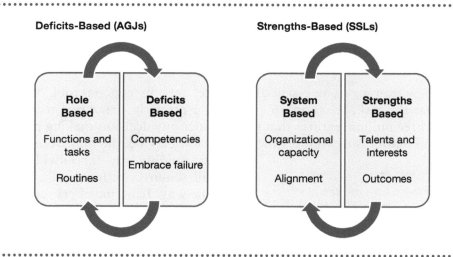

Teams

The concept of *teaming* has become an essential management tool in central and main offices, just like it has in the private sector. The organizational structure of most schools revolves around the tasks, functions, and routines of teams. If you probe administrators and teachers further on the role that teams play in their schools, however, you will find a general indifference about teaming. At times this indifference borders on open hostility to what is perceived as excessive attention to the *formation* of teams and inadequate attention to the *functioning* of teams. The school team member comments in Figure 11.4 illustrate the four pitfalls of teaming in schools.

FIGURE 11.4 THE PITFALLS OF TEAMING

PITFALL	TEAM MEMBER COMMENT	MANAGERIAL RESPONSE
Teams are designed to accomplish *managerial* goals.	"Let's devote this week to completing the district's scope and sequence charts."	"Yes, institutional requirements take priority over instructional goals."
Teams lack direction.	"What's happening with the Japanese lesson study protocol? We're supposed to be focusing on that, but we haven't even discussed it in our last three meetings."	"Yes, Nancy, I know you should be working on that. But as you know, the adoption of the common core standards has consumed most of our time. Hopefully, in a month or so, we can get back on track."
Teams do not interact effectively.	"Our team leader keeps randomly changing the timelines. We already have too much on our plates to deal with these due dates."	"I'll talk to Molly about pushing the deadlines and maybe taking some things off your plate."
Teams do not remain current.	"I've been at this for too many years to eliminate what I know are fundamental skills in algebra."	"I know a lot of the faculty agree with you, despite what the current research says. For now, let's stick with what's working."

While AGJs acknowledge the importance of teams, they perceive them as just another managerial tool to accomplish institutional goals. When a team ventures beyond the prescribed managerial boundaries, administrators will change the composition of the team or employ consultants to reorient the team towards institutional goals.

SSLs view teaming as an essential resource, not a managerial tool. No matter what the task, function, or problem, a properly structured team possesses three unique features that will enhance any decision-making process. First, no matter how well planned a decision may be, the numerous variables surrounding any schoolwide decision will require continual adjustments along the way. Team members serve that all-important feedback function.

> *SSLs view teaming as an essential resource, not a managerial tool. No matter what the task, function, or problem, a properly structured team possesses three unique features that will enhance any decision-making process.*

Second, teams provide main offices with diverse viewpoints on the merits and implementation of a particular decision. A one-size-fits-all managerial strategy is incapable of identifying and accommodating the number of variables involved in any schoolwide decision. Ultimately, effective implementation of programs or resolutions of schoolwide problems must be a creative merging of diverse ideas, experiences, and practices.

Lastly, the successful implementation of any schoolwide decision will call upon teachers and staff to be fully engaged intellectually, socially, and emotionally. If properly structured and granted the appropriate authority and environment, team members are able to self-author their personalized response to a schoolwide or team decision.

In theory, AGJs would acknowledge that all these features are valuable managerial tools. However, this is often as far as AGJs will go with the team dynamics described here—*in theory*. This is because the practical application of teaming as I have described it introduces two forces that most managerial minds prefer to avoid: uncertainty and autonomy. Both forces are in direct opposition to managerial tools designed to implement and comply.

SSLs, like their colleagues, have experienced poorly structured teams that lack strategic focus, engage in dysfunctional interpersonal communications, and ignore new sources of information and experience. SSLs, however, avoid the dysfunctionalities of poorly structured teams by carefully designing a team infrastructure that includes a shared purpose, clear direction, regulated communication, content knowledge, and administrative commitment.

Figure 11.5 outlines how an SSL would apply the attributes of effective teacher teams to the adoption of a Japanese lesson study protocol. This protocol is a method of inquiry that teacher teams employ to collaboratively author a lesson plan, observe the plan being taught, and critique the plan's execution. With any team, managerial functions and tasks are organized around a shared purpose. In schools led by AGJs, the shared purpose is an *institutional goal*, or the implementation of polices, rules, mandates, and programs. Limiting the purposes of schooling to the implementation of institutional goals establishes team structures that fail to address the two questions all teachers ask of teams they belong to:

1. Will this team make me a better teacher?

2. Will this team advance the educational goals of this school?

Without satisfactory answers to both questions, teachers will go through the motions of teaming but fail to realize the overall mission they were assigned to achieve.

FIGURE 11.5 ATTRIBUTES OF EFFECTIVE TEACHER TEAMS

ATTRIBUTES OF EFFECTIVE TEACHER TEAMS	IMPLEMENTATION OF JAPANESE LESSON STUDY
Shared purposes	Improve outcomes for students, whether focused on understandings, skills, attitudes, or engagement.
Clear goal	Bring the Japanese lesson study method of inquiry into classroom teaching practices.
Effective communication	Designate a facilitator trained in cognitive coaching for faculty teams.
Full preparation	Devote summer workshops to the study of the four phases of the Japanese lesson study.
Administrative commitment	Assign a trained teacher leader and/or administrator to each group.

In schools led by SSLs, the shared purpose is an *educational goal*, or one that seeks to develop the diverse talents, abilities, and interests of students. An agreed-upon educational purpose results in programs, training regimes, and organizational structures that *will* make better teachers and *will* advance the educational goals of the school. Defining a worthwhile purpose for teacher teaming requires an administrative commitment to providing the materials, time, space, and expertise to fulfill that agreed-upon purpose. Effective teacher teams provide SSLs with a tool for making collective sense of contemporary pedagogical theories, concepts, and practices.

Meetings

Resource 11.3 presents a taxonomy of meeting types that are convened in central and main offices. Resource 11.4 presents the roles that participants assume in each meeting type. The goals, functions, and outcomes of these meeting types fall into four broad activity structures (see Figure 11.6). Each activity structure encompasses different methods of communication, different participant roles, and different outcomes. AGJs are comfortable with meeting structures designed to implement and share information—the *telling* activity structure. Telling activity structures align perfectly with a managerial mindset that values implementation over enactment, simple over complex problem-solving, and hierarchical over flat organizational structures.

FIGURE 11.6 MEETING ACTIVITY STRUCTURES

Telling (AGJs)	Resolving (SSLs)	Gathering (SSLs)	Coaching (SSLs)
• Assigning • Assessing	• Questioning • Experimenting	• Researching • Analyzing	• Listening • Facilitating

While SSLs understand that a telling activity structure "gets stuff done," these structures don't provide the opportunity for participants to ask valued-added questions, to make collective sense of theory-based change initiatives, to develop innovative solutions to recurring schoolwide disruptions, or to create psychological safe spaces for productive collaborative interactions. To provide these opportunities, activity structures must ask meeting participants to expand their repertoire of tools to incorporate meeting types and participant roles that include researching, analyzing, listening, and facilitating. SSLs follow the meeting principles in Figure 11.7 to create these expanded versions of activity structures.

Meeting goals, functions, and outcomes are dependent on the type of meeting being held. For example, an *implementation* meeting would have very different goals, functions, and outcomes than those of a *procedural* meeting.

FIGURE 11.7 PRINCIPLES OF EXPANDED MEETING STRUCTURES

PRINCIPLE	EXPECTATION
Meeting type	Goals, functions, and outcomes of the meeting align with the targeted problem or organizational activity (see Resource 11.3).
Participant roles	Participants are clear about their roles and responsibilities when they enter the meeting (see Resource 11.4).
Psychological safety	Meeting ground rules require all participants to respect differing viewpoints.
Preparation	Participants are well prepared to assume the role they have been assigned in the meeting.
Expected outcomes	Participants are clear about how the role they play will produce the agreed-upon outcomes of the meeting.
Level of guidance	Decision-makers provide the right level of guidance throughout the meeting process.

The meeting principles followed by SSLs draw participants into a learning process with defined purposes, defined methods of inquiry, defined roles for participants, and defined outcomes. In practice, the workings of this learning process generate ongoing conversations that *figure* something out instead of merely *carrying* something out.

Master Schedule

The construction of the master schedule is another tool that will determine the level of enactment of any proposed change initiative. Every year administrators must try to reconcile competing wants, as shown in Figure 11.8.

FIGURE 11.8 MASTER SCHEDULE WANTS OVER MISSION-DRIVEN NEEDS

PERSPECTIVE	PRIORITIES
Student	• Graduation requirements • Caring teachers • Elective offerings • Extracurricular interests • Work/home commitments
Faculty	• Teaching in a particular academic major • Teaching in a certified subject area • Teaching favored ability levels • Teaching classes with few preparations • Teaching in the same room • Teaching at favored times of the day • Meeting extracurricular commitments

(Continued)

(Continued)

PERSPECTIVE	PRIORITIES
Institutional driven	• Budgets
	• Time
	• Space
	• Certification
Mission driven	• Developing the diverse talents, abilities, and interests of students
	• Helping students acquire 21st century knowledge, skills, and experiences
	• Encouraging students to become lifelong learners
	• Preparing students to excel in a complex, interconnected, and changing world
	• Fostering responsible citizenship in the global community
	• Teaching students to think critically and deeply and to assess the validity of their own thinking

AGJs approach the construction of a master schedule as a *managerial* task that prioritizes faculty and institutional-driven wants over student and mission-driven wants. SSLs approach the construction of a master schedule as an *educational* task that prioritizes student and mission-driven wants over faculty and institutional-driven wants.

Figure 11.9 lists the questions that school administrators consider during the construction of the master schedule. AGJs ask questions to ensure that the master schedule is a compliance and organizational tool. SSLs ask questions to ensure that the master schedule is an educational and aspirational tool. While there is no doubt that faculty and institutional-driven wants are necessary elements to consider when constructing the master schedule, they do not satisfy student and mission-driven wants. These wants include the ability of students to pursue personal interests, to participate in extracurricular offerings, to fulfill work and home commitments, and/or to experience mission-driven instructional platforms.

FIGURE 11.9 QUESTIONING THE MASTER SCHEDULE

QUESTIONS ASKED BY AGJs	QUESTIONS ASKED BY SSLs
• Does our master schedule adhere to organizational and faculty preferences?	• Is our master schedule student-centric?
• Does our master schedule meet course requirements for graduation?	• Is there evidence that our master schedule is placing special interests over quality educational experiences?
• Does our master schedule comply with state-mandated course requirements?	• Does our master schedule reflect a commitment to mission-driven goals?
	• Does our master schedule provide a platform for innovative approaches to curriculum and instruction?

SSL TIP
Tools in the Toolbox

AGJs excel at employing established managerial tools to perform the *how* and *what* of their offices. Every *how* and *what* issue that arrives in a main office will ultimately conform to the goals and practices of institutional schooling: Budgets will stay within line-item appropriations, personnel will perform prescribed institutional roles, teams will be assigned managerial tasks, meetings will follow prearranged agenda, and the master schedule will satisfy teacher and institutional-driven wants.

Where SSLs set themselves apart from their colleagues is in asking what mission-driven purposes each managerial tool will serve:

- Will the budget serve bottom-line institutional goals or redirect monies to address a valued educational goal?

- Will the approach to personnel be deficits-based or strengths-based?

- Will the structure of teams be organized around implementation of institutional goals or a process for advancing the educational goals of this school?

- Will meetings be called to tell administrators what to do or to make collective sense of a schoolwide problem?

- Will the development of the master schedule serve organizational wants or student wants?

Although SSLs have the same toolbox as their colleagues, the *why* of schooling is the guiding principle for how they wield those tools (see Figure 11.10).

FIGURE 11.10 GUIDING PRINCIPLES

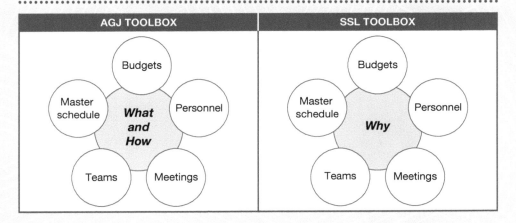

1. Of the five managerial tools described in this chapter (budgets, personnel, teams, meetings, and master schedule), which of these in your school would most influence the level of enactment of any proposed change initiative?

2. Which managerial tool(s) in your school would be most difficult to repurpose? Why?

3. Which managerial tool(s) in your school would be easiest to repurpose? Why?

4. Recent literature on organizational change targets teams and meetings as the managerial tools that are most in need of change to successfully repurpose and reorganize institutions. In thinking about the teams and meetings in your school, how would you restructure these two managerial tools in ways that would better facilitate the goals and values of change initiatives and lead to the better use of school resources?

RESOURCES

GOAL(S)	VALUES	VOCABULARIES
• Balance budget • Find additional funding	• Reduce costs • Provide best value • Maintain building facilities • Provide accountability	• Zero-based budgeting • Cost-effective • Prioritize • Fixed expenditures • Capital outlay • Contracts • Bidding • Grants • Revenues • Funds

RESOURCE 11.2   BUDGETARY COUNTERNARRATIVES

LINE ITEM	BOTTOM LINE	VALUE-ADDED LINE
Low enrollment	"Dr. Smith, have you given any thought to dropping some of your upper-course offerings? Your fourth-year German class, for example, has only six students enrolled."	"Yes, I understand the numbers in several of our upper-level courses, particularly foreign languages, are low. I brought this up with the superintendent last year and we agreed that one of the attractions of our academic program is offering four years of a foreign language. I would add that our commitment to educational excellence would be compromised by stifling a student's desire to master a foreign language."
Class size	"Dr. Smith, as you know, state funding this year has decreased. We're looking for areas to decrease expenditures. Would you consider raising your average class size? Right now, your class sizes are the lowest in the area. If we raised class size by just one student, our savings on staff would be significant."	"I'm open to exploring options for increasing class sizes in our elective courses and physical education program. However, as you know, faculty in our core academic areas are more willing to experiment with new teaching methods when class sizes are manageable."

(Continued)

(Continued)

LINE ITEM	BOTTOM LINE	VALUE-ADDED LINE
Professional development	"Dr. Smith, in looking over your budget proposal, your line item for professional conferences has risen each year. In talking with the superintendent, this is an area we agreed should be capped."	"Several of my department chairs have encouraged their teachers to present at state and national conferences. In fact, last year two of our teachers were featured speakers at the National Council of Teachers of English in Boston. I strongly support the professional development culture these department chairs are fostering."
Technology	"Dr. Smith, last year, as part of our new budgetary protocols, we established a five-year rotation schedule for the purchase of computers. The schedule we issued last year indicates that your school will be eligible for new computers in three years. In order to maintain budgetary discipline, we cannot grant your request to replace your school's computers sooner than that."	"Two years ago the district began revising its curriculum to emphasize real-world problems in each discipline. With the expertise of Dr. Horik, our consultant for this project, our teachers have created cases that immerse students in real-world scenarios, requiring them to access various databases to create solutions. As I stated in my proposal, Dr. Horik and our team determined that our current computers are missing essential components necessary for students to access, analyze, and synthesize data to address their assigned real-world problems."

RESOURCE 11.3 TAXONOMY OF MEETING TYPES

MEETING TYPE/PURPOSE	PARTICIPANTS (Optimum #)	CHARACTERISTICS	OUTCOMES
Implementation Execute policy, procedure, program, or mandate	• Decision-maker • Implementors (1–3 Participants)	Discussing: • Budgets • Systems • Schedules • Personnel • Materials • Space Providing feedback: • Listening • Correcting • Adapting • Guiding	• Action plans • Institutionalization • Clarification • Strategy

MEETING TYPE/PURPOSE	PARTICIPANTS (Optimum #)	CHARACTERISTICS	OUTCOMES
Procedural Redesign system	• Decision-maker • Contributors • Executors (3–5 Participants)	• Identifying problem with standard routine • Asking what we know about problem • Identifying options • Creating a plan of action	• Rule • Protocol • Revision of SOP
Problem Resolve organizational problem	• Decision-maker • Consultants • Contributors • Implementors (5–7 Participants)	• Identifying the problem • Determining what is the type of problem (simple, complicated, complex) • Identifying what is known about the problem • Identifying what patterns exist • Identifying what variances exist • Establishing hypothesis • Creating plan of action • Testing plan • Revising plan of action	• Reauthoring of aims–goals–functions • Reconfiguring organizational structure • Reassigning personnel • Executing training regime
New initiative Adopt new program	• Decision-maker • Consultants • Contributors • Implementors • Targeted groups (5–7 Participants)	• Establish rational for new initiative: situation–strategy–capacity • Establish alignment with school instructional worldview • Create plan of action	• Allocation of resources • System redesign • Organizational redesign • Adoption of new materials • Employment of consultants • Changed supervisory stance • Training regime

RESOURCE 11.4 ROLES OF MEETING PARTICIPANTS

PARTICIPANT	ROLE	FUNCTIONS
Decision-maker	Individual chairing meeting and determining strategy	• Set agenda • Manage agenda/meeting • Invite participants • Gather relevant data • Prepare position paper • Coach participants
Consultants	Individual(s) knowledgeable about the causes, theories, and strategies governing the problem	• Develop and deliver presentation on relevant theories, concepts, and strategies
Contributors	Individual(s) most knowledgeable about the practical aspects of the problem and who understand the day-to-day implications of agreed-upon strategies	• Present day-to-day implications of proposed strategies • Offer practical options from their experience with the problem
Implementors	Individual(s) responsible for implementing strategies	• Ask clarifying questions • Identify potential problems with implementation

CHAPTER 12

....

VIEW FROM
THE BALCONY

In this chapter I describe the two views of a school organization. AGJs view their organization from the schoolhouse floor. The problems they see and the strategies they employ concentrate on managing the disorders located on the floor of the school. SSLs do not view any schoolwide problem or change initiative as an isolated disorder to be fixed with a managerial tool. SSLs view all schoolwide problems as a mix of controllable and uncontrollable variables. To make collective sense of these variables, SSLs go up to the metaphorical balconies of their schools to see patterns that emerge from big-picture views of the schoolhouse floor. The emerging patterns serve as a source for possible strategies and managerial tools to achieve a mission-driven goal.

> **The best CEOs also find ways to maintain a view from the balcony so they can see patterns, find hope on the horizon, and look for opportunities.**
>
> —Dewar et al. (2022)

Each chapter in this book describes managerial and leadership tools that school administrators wield to competently manage school operations. I draw a distinction between how AGJs and SSLs apply these tools in their schools: AGJs employ tools to comply with institutional goals; SSLs employ the same tools to pursue mission-driven goals. When these managerial tools are used on the schoolhouse floor, *how* they are applied depends on where school administrators stand in their schools.

AGJs remain standing on the floors of their schools when they respond to schoolwide problems and enact change initiatives. The tools and strategies they employ concentrate on successfully managing the particulars of fixing a problem or implementing a change initiative. SSLs, on the other hand, do not view schoolwide problems as isolated events to be fixed with managerial tools, nor do they use these tools to merely implement change initiatives.

SSLs view all schoolwide problems and change initiatives as a convergence of numerous controllable and uncontrollable social, emotional, organizational, and educational variables. To make collective sense of these colliding variables, SSLs climb to the balcony of their schools to acquire a big-picture view of the managerial tools at their disposal and to assess how to use these tools to solve problems and enact change initiatives while remaining faithful to the educational mission of their schools.

Looking down from the balcony upon a schoolhouse floor, SSLs see these colliding social, emotional, organizational, and educational variables and disentangle and reconnect them into recognizable patterns using the strategies outlined here.

STRATEGIES SSLs USE TO PREPARE DIFFERENTLY

- SSLs admit to educational wrongs.
- SSLs self-author a personalized instructional worldview.
- SSL actualize what is important.
- SSLs do their homework.

The patterns that emerge from big-picture views of the schoolhouse floor serve as a foundation for possible strategies and as a guide for wielding managerial tools to achieve mission-driven goals.

SSLs PREPARE DIFFERENTLY

Along with the managerial courses that prepare school administrators to run a school well, an SSL also self-authors an instructional worldview of schooling that orginates from academic critiques of the goals and practices of institutional education. These critiques challenge the beliefs and practices of institutional schooling and its current configurations.

SSLs Admit to Educational Wrongs

In private, and at times in public, SSLs will question the beliefs and practices of institutional schooling (see Resource 12.1). For the most part, the public is satisfied with the goals, practices, and configurations of institutional schooling. Parents accept that

- the goal of schooling is certification,
- children learn best by listening,
- academic subjects are the knowledge of most worth,
- the organization of knowledge should be subject centered,
- student understanding is best assessed by a test, and
- effective teaching is the transmission of information to students by a knowledgeable teacher.

SSLs question all these assumptions of institutional schooling. They develop counternarratives to these assumptions and, given the right community and institutional situations, enact policies, programs, and organizational configurations that better conform to how children learn and what children will need to know to be able to function in the world we inhabit. SSLs believe the following:

- The goal of schooling is to develop the diverse talents, interests, and abilities of children and adolescents.
- Children learn best in environments that require the active, constructive involvement of the learner.
- Children learn best when they participate in activities that are perceived to be useful in real life and are culturally relevant.
- Good assessments move beyond "one right answer" instruments to authentic products that challenge students to examine the possibilities inherent in open-ended, complex problems.
- Effective teaching happens when the teacher helps a student relate their own experiences to the broader principles and concepts of a discipline or many disciplines.
- Classrooms should be places where students spend a lot of time discussing concepts, themes, and problems with teachers and peers.

SSLs Self-Author a Personalized Instructional Worldview

SSLs continually question beliefs about the *what*, *why*, and *how* of schooling. The result of this deep inquiry is used to author an educational worldview based on a personal vision of what it means to be educated, what administrative tools should be employed to realize that vision, and what the SSL's role will be in achieving that vision. Figure 12.1 offers SSLs prompts for articulating their own educational worldview. I encourage you to take some time with Figure 12.1 to write in your educational worldviews.

FIGURE 12.1 AUTHORING AN EDUCATIONAL WORLDVIEW

QUESTION	CONCEPTS	WHAT I BELIEVE (My Worldview)
What are the goals of schooling?	• Is there an ultimate goal or multiple goals? • What goals (vocational, civic, self-developmental, humanistic, institutional) should our school pursue?	
How do children learn?	• Imitation • Association • Student interest • Pursuit of important questions of life	
What do all children need to know?	• Great books • Basic skills • Cognitive processes • Disciplinary concepts • Contemporary problems	
How should we organize subject matter?	• Textbooks • Disciplinary representations • Test preparation manuals • Themes • Problems • Concepts • Big ideas • What draws a student to a subject	

QUESTION	CONCEPTS	WHAT I BELIEVE (My Worldview)
How should we assess understanding of subject matter?	• Tests • Grades • School projects • Performances • Authentic products	
How should we teach?	• Lecture • Model • Direct instruction • Socratic questioning • Facilitate/coach	
How should we work with children?	• Pay attention to incentives (rewards and punishments) • Pay attention to developmental stages (cognitive/emotional) • Convey that routines and rules are important for real-world success. • Honor individual differences/talents/interests • Include moral training • Determine if rebellion is normal/abnormal	

SSL Actualize What Is Important

There are a multitude of complex social, emotional, intellectual, and organizational relationships in every school. When standing on the schoolhouse floor, it is often difficult to make sense of how these relationships interact with each other. From their position on the school balcony, SSLs determine which relationships are important. They articulate how these relationships interact with each other and then design systems and organizational configurations to accommodate the important relationships. Figure 12.2 is an example of how an SSL might clarify for teachers what is important, what systems in the organization will actualize what is important, and what established procedures and plans will advance and enhance these processes.

> *From their position on the school balcony, SSLs determine which relationships are important. They articulate how these relationships interact with each other and then design systems and organizational configurations to accommodate the important relationships.*

FIGURE 12.2   HOW SSLs ACTUALIZE WHAT IS IMPORTANT

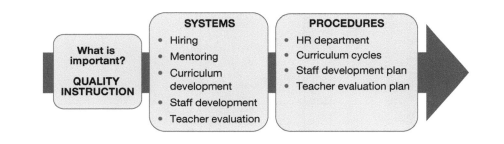

SSLs Do Their Homework

There is not a problem or issue in schooling today that has not been well researched. Libraries and a host of databases contain professional journals, blogs, and governmental studies that have closely examined the efficacy of programs, policies, theories, and practices directly related to the *how*, *what*, and *why* of schooling. From school violence to effective bilingual programs, there have been numerous studies of what works, how it works, and why it works. Many of these studies have brought into question the effectiveness of well-established school configurations, policies, and instructional methodologies that are in opposition to what the research says are best practices.

AGJs assume that the programs, policies, and instructional methodologies they are asked to implement have already been thoroughly researched and sanctioned, and so they see little value in reading research studies. Even if they were to have doubts about the efficacy of a program, policy, or practice, many do not have sufficient theoretical backgrounds to question or modify what their administrative colleagues have accepted as an established organizational or instructional truth.

SSLs never accept an alleged educational truth at face value. No matter how firmly embedded that truth may be on the schoolhouse floor, they will climb to the schoolhouse balcony to investigate the theoretical justifications and practical applications of that truth. No matter how impressive a program may appear—whole language instruction, language immersion, drug resistance education, the power of GRIT (growth, resilience, integrity, and tenacity)—SSLs will seek out the truths of that program in the academic community.

SSLs THINK DIFFERENTLY

AGJs enter school buildings responding to specific questions about functions, tasks, and events. SSLs enter school buildings asking big questions about the goals, methods, and nature of schooling. Asking big questions moves conversations from the certainties of managerial functions to the uncertainties of numerous known and unknown variables that interact in unpredictable ways.

SSLs Ask Big Questions

Managing the day-to-day operations of a school involves answering specific questions about given functions, tasks, and events:

- Will we be on Assembly B schedule on Friday?
- When will the bathroom on the third floor be fixed?
- How many days will the state testing program last?
- Whom do I see about changing my chaperone assignment?
- When are we changing over to the new grading program?
- Whom should I see about my reimbursement for the NCTM conference?

While all these questions asked on the schoolhouse floor are relevant to the smooth running of a school, and are questions that AGJs are ready to answer, they are not the same questions that SSLs ask while standing on the schoolhouse balcony. SSLs ask big questions about the goals, the methods, and the nature of schooling:

- What is our educational vision?
- What knowledge is of most worth?

- What motivates children and adolescents to learn?

- Should all students study the same academic curriculum?

- Does our school provide opportunities to develop talents and interests outside of tested subjects?

- What do standardized tests really measure?

- What existing practices should we question?

- Should a school be designed to fit the child, or do we make the child fit the school?

- Are the current accountability mandates enhancing mission-driven goals and values?

Each of these big questions asks school community members to examine their beliefs and assumptions about schooling. Some members may answer these questions with institutional responses such as, "Algebra is the gateway to a well-paying job." SSLs make use of formal and informal school communication opportunities to introduce different philosophies and models of schooling that are the foundation for continuous improvement and the source of all innovative approaches to schooling, teaching, and learning.

The informational component of answering big questions is essential to any introduction of new policies, programs, or practices. Not until SSLs are satisfied that a school community understands the *why* of a change initiative do they proceed with the *what* and *how*. Even when SSLs feel the *why* has been satisfied, they are careful to craft programs, policies, and practices that will work at the margins of a schoolhouse floor without disrupting the entire floor.

SSLs Are Comfortable With Ambiguity

When you spend most of your time on the schoolhouse floor, all problems appear to be simple: There is an identifiable cause, there is a managerial tool to fix the cause, and there are prescribed managerial steps to implement the fix. Standing on the schoolhouse balcony, SSLs view all schoolwide problems—from academic to behavioral—as the interaction of multiple school and community variables, some of which are controllable, but most of which are not.

Solving a simple schoolwide problem is merely a matter of selecting a managerial tool or tools, developing a plan of action, and delegating an administrator to implement the plan. Complex problems, however, require administrators to participate in a method of inquiry that, at a minimum, would include answers to the following questions:

- What is the situation?

- What do we know about the situation?

- What outcomes do we want from the situation?

- What do we do?

- How do we do it?

- How do we know if it works?

- What do we do next?

AGJs would view this entire inquiry process as a large distraction from implementing a mangerial routine to address a schoolwide problem. SSLs view this inquiry into schoolwide problems as a powerful means to improve best practices and standard operating procedures.

SSLs Are Curious

Looking down on the schoolhouse floor, SSLs notice deviations from organizational and classroom norms. They are attracted to unique organizational structures and teaching methods that connect what we know about how children learn to mission-driven goals and values. When these pockets of innovation are spotted, SSLs return to the schoolhouse floor to develop strategies that will transform these pockets into instructional norms. Depending upon the social and institutional context of the community SSLs find themselves in, they would select and develop one or more of the elements shown in Figure 12.3 to multiply pockets of innovation. A pivotal element in spreading pockets of innovation is the SSL's readiness to work with teachers on the schoolhouse floor to author and implement innovative approaches to teaching and learning.

FIGURE 12.3 CREATING POCKETS OF INNOVATION

Personnel		Champions Mentors Consultants
Structural		Curriculum reconfiguration Learning communities Staff development
Institutional		Teacher performance plans Accountability mandates Benchmarks

SSLs Are Student Centered

The schoolhouse floor is littered with assumptions and practices that support and advance institutional goals, such as standardization, documentation, accountability, and cost-effectiveness. Contrary to these institutional assumptions and practices, school mission statements promote student-centered goals and values: questioning, exploring, engagement, and personal development. SSLs author narratives and develop organizational and pedagogical practices that offer alternatives to institutional assumptions. These narratives might include the following:

- Children learn best when they are given the opportunity to pursue a personal interest or goal. In action, this means valuing interests more than requirements.

- Children learn best by doing. In action this means valuing practice more than listening.

- Children learn best by failure. In action, this means valuing feedback more than right answers.

- Children learn best from stories and real-world problems. In action, this means valuing knowledge more than information.

SSLs Solve Problems

Those who spend most of their time on the schoolhouse floor develop a short-term mindset: Fix the crisis of the day and move on to the next crisis. Established managerial tools—policies, procedures, rules, programs— lend themselves well to short-term fixes. AGJs employ these established managerial tools to fix a problem or implement a change initiative. Their primary motive is to complete a task—move paper, or a problem, or an initiative off their desks to make room for the next notice, or problem, or initiative.

> *SSLs standing on the balcony see patterns of behavior and practices composed of numerous known and unknown variables that interact in unpredictable ways.*

SSLs standing on the balcony see patterns of behavior and practices composed of numerous known and unknown variables that interact in unpredictable ways. Fixes to a variable or variables using established managerial tools may address a schoolhouse problem in the short term but will not solve the problem in the long term. SSLs disrupt patterns of behavior and practices with structural and pedagogical changes that work at changing the mindset of students and teachers on the schoolhouse floor. Figure 12.4 provides examples of fixes versus solutions to schoolwide problems. Changing the mindset of a school community is a long-term process of educating—the *why* and *what* of goals—and then enacting—the *how* and *who* of implementation.

FIGURE 12.4 SOLVING SCHOOLWIDE PROBLEMS

SCHOOLWIDE PROBLEM	FIXING THE PROBLEM	SOLVING THE PROBLEM
Student absenteeism	"Three strikes and you're out" policy	Establish alternative schooling configurations
Student behavior problem	Detentions	Design disciplinary program based on positive discipline
Low test scores	Test-prep program	Redesign curriculum offerings in targeted areas
Tardiness	Grade deduction	Begin instruction at the bell
Fighting	Suspension/expulsion	Structure supervision based on the theory of unowned places
Drugs	DARE program	Expand counseling services

SSLs LEAD DIFFERENTLY

For an administrator standing on the schoolhouse floor, leadership is reduced to the managerial functions of adjusting policies, procedures, processes, and systems (the *how*) to produce certain outcomes (the *what*). AGJs are experts at performing these managerial functions. Standing on the schoolhouse balcony, however, SSLs see patterns of behavior that have remained resistant to managerial fixes. Leading from the schoolhouse balcony draws the school community into questioning the purposes, goals, values, and practices of what administrators, teachers, and students are doing on the schoolhouse floor.

SSLs Start With Asking *Why?*

The questions that emerge on the schoolhouse floor are *how* and *what* questions: adjusting policies, procedures, processes, and systems (*how*) to produce certain outcomes (*what*). AGJs are experts at the implementation function, this *how* and *what* of management. Those who spend most of their time standing on the schoolhouse floor allow the *how* and *what* questions of running a school to reduce the leadership function to instrumental responses to daily *what* and *how* problems.

When school administrators positions themselves on the schoolhouse balcony, they catch glimpses of *how* and *what* problems and are also exposed to *why* questions, such as, "*Why* do these problems keep arising?" For SSLs, solving a schoolwide problem begins with discovering the source of the problem, which draws the school community into questioning the purposes, the goals, the values, and the practices of what administrators, teachers, and students are doing on the schoolhouse floor.

SSLs Know the Territory

No school culture or community is a blank slate. Although all schools have similar organizational and instructional profiles, they exhibit distinct patterns of behavior and expectations that originate from the community's socioeconomic makeup, from significant events and achievements, and from colorful personalities. These cultural inputs are often woven together into a story illustrating the goals and the values of that particular school.

When AGJs enter a particular school culture, they respond in one of two ways: They either ignore it or pander to it. In the former stance, they apply policies, procedures, rules, and programs that will normalize the particularities of a school culture. In the latter stance, they apply the same policies, procedures, rules, and programs in ways that magnify the particulars of a school culture.

Standing on the schoolhouse floor, SSLs view the particulars of a school culture as a necessary means for a school community to make collective sense of the purposes and methods of the school they teach in or send their children to. Standing on the schoolhouse balcony, however, they see how the particulars of a school culture can hinder achieving the valued ends of schooling.

SSLs navigate the particulars of a school culture by looking for cracks in the boundaries of those particulars. When they find those cracks, they insert policies, procedures, rules, or programs that maintain some semblance of the particulars but at the same time redefine those particulars in a way that enhances a valued end of schooling. In the process of finding and then enlarging the cracks in the particulars of a school culture, SSLs are careful not to eradicate the boundary altogether. Both their legitimacy as a school leader and their ability to navigate between different cultural boundaries are wholly dependent on a school community's faith in the preservation of its members' experiences of how schools should look and operate.

SSLs Focus on the Right Things

Each day the schoolhouse floor is littered with managerial, behavioral, and educational problems that end up on main office calendars. AGJs look at their calendars each morning and identify what functions and tasks they will address. These tasks and functions fall into one of three categories: instrumental, educational, or creative (see Figure 12.5). While AGJs tell school communities that the role they value most is instructional leadership—the educational and creative functions—those functions and tasks are usually delegated or moved to another day. What remains on their calendars are the instrumental functions of school administration.

FIGURE 12.5 FOCUS OF CALENDAR ENTRIES IN MAIN OFFICES

INSTRUMENTAL (The *How* and *Who*)	EDUCATIONAL (The *What* and *Why*)	CREATIVE (The *Ought*)
Systems	Mission statement	Vision
Personnel	Programs	Theories, ideas, concepts
Budgets	Course configurations	Problem–solution fits
Materials	Master schedules	Experts
Time	Curriculum handbook	Models
Space	Staff development	Experimentation
Expertise	Professional performance	Risk-taking

SSLs look at their daily calendars from the schoolhouse balcony. From that vantage point, the instrumental functions of running a school are simply the background, allowing the focus to be on educational and creative functions that advance mission-driven goals and values. This focus on educational and creative functions does not mean that instrumental functions are absent from main office calendars. Educational and creative functions are empty processes without the foundation of a well-run school. SSLs view the instrumental functions listed on their calendars as opportunities to pursue organizational or instructional routines in ways that redefine beliefs and values about teaching and learning.

SSLs Influence

The fundamental dilemma that all school leaders confront is finding the right balance between changes that support existing cultural norms and changes that are transformative. The former always involves some form of consent; the latter involves some form of coercion. AGJs highly value the level of cooperation and high morale that results from changes that support organizational and instructional norms.

While SSLs see the same value in high morale and cooperation, from their balcony view they spot organizational and instructional norms that are serving as obstacles to achieving mission-driven goals and practices. They negotiate the balance between stability and transformation through a series of administrative moves that influence the direction and substance of a change initiative (see Resource 12.2). Each move is orchestrated in a way that replaces regulative measures—standardized tests, observation protocols—with normative measures that respect and enhance teachers' sense of the valued ends of schooling and agree with their preexisting instructional beliefs and practices.

SSLs Establish and Enforce Norms

At the same time SSLs author professional teaching norms, they clearly articulate behaviors and performance standards that will be regulated. Any behavior or practice that would humiliate, injure, or evidence pedagogical malpractice is addressed with appropriate administrative processes and sanctions.

SSLs Enact Frameworks

On the schoolhouse floor, AGJs treat all mandates, programs, policies, and procedures as functions of implementation: plan → tasks → execution → documentation. All aspects of the implementation are controlled by a series of managerial routines, such as budgets, timelines, and resource allocation.

Standing on the balcony, SSLs articulate a framework for each task and function. AGJs, for example, could treat staff development as merely a matter of scheduling workshops, hiring consultants, distributing materials, and collecting feedback questionnaires. SSLs, on the other hand, ask themselves what training framework to adopt to best assist staff with making collective sense of new pedagogical theories and practices. An *implementation* framework is populated with a lot of telling, script following, and documentation. A *coaching* framework articulated by an SSL would include the following:

- designing a method of training for coaches
- identifying the specifics of key coaching practices and routines
- integrating the coaching model into diverse learning contexts
- identifying how coaches will interact with teachers

Whether for curriculum development, teacher evaluation, textbook adoption, or the master schedule creation, SSLs author a framework that not only prescribes the *how* and *what* of the administrative function but, more importantly, joins that *how* and *what* to a mission-driven *why* of schooling.

SSLs Take Risks

The avoidance of any form of uncertainty on the schoolhouse floor is embedded in the managerial mindset of AGJs. They create organizational infrastructures composed of policies, procedures, rules, schedules, and systems to ensure certainty in how their schools function and how teachers, staff, and students behave. Deviations from these organizational and behavioral norms are responded to with a sanction or the implementation of a new policy, procedure, rule, schedule, or system.

These managerial certainties imposed on the schoolhouse floor project the image of a well-run school doing things well. Viewed from the schoolhouse balcony, the movement of students, the teaching of subject matter, the documentation of academic achievement, and the behavior of student populations all represent the certainties of institutional values: compliance, standards, rules, routines, and conformity. SSLs notice from the schoolhouse balcony that little to no attention is paid to educational goals and values written in school mission statements: agency, interests, relationships, novelty, and originality.

Disrupting and repurposing the certainties on the schoolhouse floor to pursue mission-driven goals and values involves a level of risk and uncertainty that AGJs are unwilling to take. But although their schools are *doing things well*, they may not be *doing the right things*.

SSL TIP
Eclectic Leadership

AGJs comfortably operate from the schoolhouse floor, adeptly utilizing established managerial tools to address emerging needs. Each *what* prompts an institutional *how*—resource allocation, personnel management, rule creation, or system adjustment—aimed at maintaining efficient, predictable, quantifiable, and accountable organizational structures. AGJs excel at applying managerial tools that competently perform the *what* and *how* of their schools' operations. By standing on the schoolhouse floor, they miss these balcony views of the big picture of schooling:

- patterns of student and teacher behavior

- responsiveness to cultural diversity

- development of individual talents, abilities, and interests

- pockets of organizational and instructional innovation

- decaying professional norms

- dysfunctional systems

- emerging troubles in student welfare

- pedagogical effectiveness

Of course, SSLs aim to operate their schools well from the schoolhouse floor by *doing things well*. But at the same time they seek to *do the right things* based on what they see from the schoolhouse balcony. SSLs achieve this by constantly moving between the schoolhouse floor—the *how* and *what* of operations—to the schoolhouse balcony—the

(Continued)

(Continued)

> *SSLs aim to operate their schools well from the schoolhouse floor by doing things well. But at the same time they seek to do the right things based on what they see from the schoolhouse balcony.*

why of educating. SSLs employ a diverse set of leadership and managerial roles to embed the *why* of schooling—the balcony view—into the *what* and *how* of schooling—the floor view. When positioned on the schoolhouse floor, an SSL assumes the role of leader and manager, implementing the *what* and *how* of an agreed-upon strategy. When positioned on the schoolhouse balcony, an SSL assumes the role of champion and inventor, authoring a new *why* of schooling. Unlike their main office colleagues, SSLs view all schoolwide problems from the balcony first, addressing the *why* of schooling, and then embed that *why* into the roles and functions of eclectic leadership. Figure 12.6 summarizes the different leadership and managerial roles that an eclectic leader would assume when moving between the schoolhouse floor and balcony.

FIGURE 12.6 ECLECTIC LEADERSHIP

ROLE	PROCESS	TASKS
What leaders do (direct)	Plan → facilitate → build capacity	• Organize • Model • Monitor • Redesign
What managers do (implement)	Tell → allocate → inspect	• Standardize • Schedule • Allocate • Follow up
What inventors do (author)	Theorize → hypothesize → experiment	• Question • Gather data • Postulate • Imagine • Test • Design
What champions do (advocate)	Disrupt → purpose → enact	• Challenge • Purpose • Educate • Authorize

1. What are some common administrative responses to a problem on the schoolhouse floor? What would be a balcony response to those same problems?

2. What mix of educational and career experiences would prepare you for making sense out of balcony views of schoolwide problems?

3. In thinking about the administrative meetings you attend, why is it rare for big questions to be considered at these meetings?

4. What mix of managerial and leadership skills would you need to move between the schoolhouse floor and balcony?

RESOURCES

RESOURCE 12.1   THE GOALS OF SCHOOLING

SCHOOL FUNCTION	INSTITUTIONAL GOALS	EDUCATIVE GOALS
The goal is . . .	Preparing for occupational roles	Expanding the intellect
Learning is. . . .	Acquiring information	Constructing meaning
Teaching is . . .	Transmitting information	Facilitating understanding
Pedagogy is . . .	Implementing the technique of the day	Inquiring
Subject matter content is . . .	Complying with state standards	Providing real-life problems
Performance is . . .	Attaining high scores on standardized tests	Solving authentic problems

RESOURCE 12.2   INFLUENCING

MOVE	WHAT SSLs DO
Purpose rather than implement	They give voice to a narrative that informs the school community of gaps existing between schoolwide norms and mission-driven goals and values. (See Figure 7.5)
Adapt rather than adopt	They edit the beliefs, theories, and practices of a change initiative to fit the preexisting beliefs and practices of their faculty. (See introduction to Chapter 6.)
Align rather than impose	They redefine institutional goals and practices to align with mission-driven goals and practices. (See "Three Strikes and You're Out" vignette in Chapter 2.)
Engage rather than transmit	They develop training regimes that provide teachers with a sustained professional development consisting of close interaction with colleagues and one-to-one interaction with trained coaches. (See Resource 8.2.)
Reinforce rather than fragment	They select a core of instructional methodologies that become the norms of classroom practice. (See Figure 12.1.)

CHAPTER 13

....

THE REALITIES OF SCHOOLING

In this chapter I discuss the institutional realities of schooling, or what has been termed the "grammar of schooling." SSLs set themselves apart from their colleagues in school offices by looking for and exploiting cracks in the grammar of schooling to implement organizational configurations that restore the values written into school mission statements.

The role of the leaders is to define reality and give hope.

—Ken Chenault in Dewar et al. (2022)

THE INSTITUTIONAL REALITY OF SCHOOLING

In John Goodlad's seminal study of instructional programs in thirteen high schools throughout the country, he described observing the following regularities of classroom practice:

> [I saw] the teacher explaining or lecturing to the total class or a single student, occasionally asking questions requiring factual answers; the teacher, when not lecturing, observing or monitoring students working individually at their desks; students listening or appearing to listen to the teacher and occasionally responding to the teacher's questions; students working individually at their desks on reading or writing assignments; and all with little emotion, from interpersonal warmth to expressions of hostility. (Goodlad, 1984, p. 230)

Researchers would later coin the phrase the *grammar of schooling* (Tyack & Tobin, 1994) to label the dominate organizational and pedagogical structures of schooling in this nation (see Resource 13.1). These organizational and pedagogical structures create, in the words of Jackson (1968), the "facts of classroom life" for students attending our public school systems (see Figure 13.1). Those walking through most schools today will find that not much has changed since Goodlad's research was published forty years ago.

FIGURE 13.1 THE FACTS OF LIFE IN OUR NATION'S CLASSROOMS

EDUCATIONAL ASPECT	CHARACTERISTICS
School setting	• Crowds • Rules • Uniform movement • Hierarchies of power (principal → teacher → student) • Short, fixed-length blocks of time • Individual classrooms
Classroom setting	• Delays • Denial of desire • Interruptions • Praise or blame
Instruction	• Telling • Taking notes • Reciting • Assigning • Reading textbooks • Testing • Grading • Covering content
Students' adaptive styles	• Being patient • Playing the game ("doing school") • Cutting school • Rebelling (for placement in special education)

The grammar of schooling is founded on the following assumptions about teaching and learning:

- Learning takes place in the mind, not the body.

- All children learn, or should learn, in the same way.

- All children should learn the same subject matter.

- Learning takes place in the classroom, not in the world.

- Knowledge is inherently fragmented.

- Knowledge exists outside the child.

- Schools communicate the truth.

- Learning is primarily individualistic.

- Competition accelerates learning.

- Standardized tests are the best way to assess what has been learned.

- All knowledge can be found in textbooks.

These institutional assumptions about teaching and learning have been translated by main offices into the following managerial beliefs about the *what* and *how* of schooling:

- The goals of schooling are answers to technical questions: How do we best deliver a service or implement a program?

- Education is training.

- Knowledge is scientifically proven.

- Learning occurs when all students complete the same assignments at the same time with the same outcomes.

- Teaching and learning can be measured, predicted, and controlled.

- Teaching is management of children and curriculum.

- Curriculum development aligns course content with state standards and state testing instruments.

- A test measures knowledge.

- Schools are best organized around prescribed time periods, subjects, and departments.

The reality of institutional schooling is dominated by the grammar of schooling and a managerial mindset aimed at enforcing the institutional goals of standardization, accountability, and quantification. AGJs have become experts at implementing policies, procedures, programs, and organizational configurations that standardize curriculum and teaching methodologies, hold teachers and students accountable for achieving common standards and prescribed pedagogical practices, and rely on data to inform the decision-making in main offices.

THE EDUCATIONAL HOPE OF SCHOOLING

In the early 1900sa group of progressive educators (Cremin, 1961) described a different reality of schooling (see Resource 13.2) founded on the following assumptions about teaching and learning:

- Students are active producers of knowledge rather than passive recipients.

- Students learn best when they can engage in experiential learning aligned with their personal goals.

- Students learn best by doing rather than receiving information.

- Students learn best when skills, concepts, and products are woven together rather than taught in sequence.

- Students learn best when they receive frequent and specific feedback on real-world applications.

- Students learn best in collaborative venues.

- Real-world problems should guide instruction.

- Final products should be connected to real-world domains.

These educational assumptions about teaching and learning are rarely acknowledged in main offices. AGJs often lack the instructional vocabularies, conceptual frameworks, and organizational configurations to accommodate the following educational beliefs about the *why* of schooling:

- Goals of schooling are answers to aspirational questions: How do we best develop the diverse talents, abilities, and interests of students?

- Education is transformative.

- Knowledge is constructed.

- Learning occurs when students are asked to apply knowledge in diverse and authentic contexts, explain ideas, interpret texts, predict phenomena, and construct arguments based on evidence.

- Teaching and learning are processes of questioning, discovering, modeling, applying, and creating.

- Teaching is providing students with a variety of information sources (technological and conceptual).

- Curriculum development should include creating learning situations that help students elaborate on or restructure their current knowledge.

- Students should produce authentic products judged by professionals in the field.

- Curricula are best organized around big questions, problems, concepts, or themes.

Although the grammar of schooling continues to dominate the policy and organizational landscape in our nation's schools, pockets of progressive schooling exist that are aimed at the educational goals of autonomy, creativity, and growth. SSLs set themselves apart from their colleagues in main offices by looking for and exploiting cracks in the grammar of schooling to create these pockets by implementing policies, procedures, programs, and organizational configurations that redefine the institutional meanings of the values written into school mission statements.

> *Although the grammar of schooling continues to dominate the policy and organizational landscape in our nation's schools, pockets of progressive schooling exist that are aimed at the educational goals of autonomy, creativity, and growth.*

SSL TIP

The Global Reality of Schooling

AGJs pay little attention to the dueling realities of schooling. They have spent their careers honing managerial skills that maintain the smooth running of school systems designed to produce students that have been well socialized into performing occupational roles that value attendance, punctuality, following orders, completing assignments on time, and performing explicitly assigned duties. The century-old grammar of schooling perfectly mirrors the values and practices of manufacturing and managerial occupations.

This grammar of schooling, however, has become obsolete in a global, social, economic, political, and intellectual environment that values creativity, flexibility, collaboration, critical thinking, and entrepreneurship (see Figure 13.2). Employers in the global marketplace are looking for individuals who have developed dispositions and habits of thought that are in direct opposition to the dispositions and habits of thought of industrial-era employees. Employers today want individuals that question orders; work on problems, not assignments; move around different work venues; network; take risks; and frequently cross disciplinary boundaries.

FIGURE 13.2   REDEFINING VALUES

VALUE	INDUSTRIAL	GLOBAL MARKETPLACE
Autonomy	Conformity	Agency
Diversity	Imitators	Creators
Success	Performance	Growth
Knowledge and skills	Prescribed	Emergent
Competence	Know how	Know why
Personalization	Track	Self-author
Teaching	Transmitter	Facilitator

(Continued)

(Continued)

Although numerous research studies, books, and governmental reports have documented the disconnect between the grammar of schooling and global knowledge, skills, and dispositions, few schools have redesigned their organizational structures and pedagogical practices to better prepare their students to succeed in a global economic, political, and social environment. These gaps exist, and will continue to exist, in schools led by AGJs whose academic backgrounds, managerial experiences, career opportunities, and community support are governed by the successful implementation of institutional goals and practices—the grammar of schooling. The best hope for future generations of children lies with schools led by SSLs who have the courage to expose the reality of institutional schooling and the vision and skills to author a new definition of the grammar of schooling (see Resource 13.1).

> *The best hope for future generations of children lies with schools led by SSLs who have the courage to expose the reality of institutional schooling and the vision and skills to author a new definition of the grammar of schooling.*

REFLECTIVE QUESTIONS

1. What are the institutional realities of schooling that are serving as obstacles to realizing the educational hope of schooling?

2. In your school, what cracks in the grammar of schooling could your administrative team exploit to implement policies, procedures, programs, and organizational configurations that would pursue the educational hope of schooling?

3. What changes in your school organization or classroom instruction could you point to that are preparing your students for their place in a global marketplace?

RESOURCES

RESOURCE 13.1   THE GRAMMAR OF SCHOOLING

LEARNING COMPONENT	OLD GRAMMAR OF SCHOOLING	REDEFINED GRAMMAR OF SCHOOLING
Purpose	Assimilate preexisting content	Engage student as producer in a variety of fields and worthy human pursuits
View of knowledge	Siloed and fixed	Constructed, interconnected, and dynamic
Learning modality	Teaching as transmission	Learning through doing, apprenticeships
Roles	One teacher, many students	Vertically integrated communities: teachers, students as teachers, and field members providing expertise
Boundaries between disciplines	Rigid	Flexible
Boundaries between school and real world	Rigid	Flexible
Places where students learn	Schools	Various community centers (including schools), field sites, online
Selection of subjects	Limited	Open, multiple pathways based on student interests and needs
Time	Short blocks of fixed length	Longer, variable blocks that provide time for immersive experiences
Space	Individual classrooms	Linked spaces, variable spaces
Assessment	Seat time, standardized tests	Creation of worthy products in the domain: projects, portfolios, performances, research
Organizational	Linear, top-down planning	Distributed leadership, spiral of inquiry
Stance toward community	Defensive, keeping out	Welcoming, inviting in

RESOURCE 13.2   21ST CENTURY OCCUPATIONAL SKILLS

THE FOUR Cs OF 21ST CENTURY LEARNING Trilling and Fadel (2009)	
• Creativity • Critical thinking • Communication • Collaboration	

TONY WAGNER'S SEVEN SURVIVAL SKILLS Wagner (2008)	
• Critical thinking and problem-solving • Collaboration across networks • Agility and adaptability • Initiative and entrepreneurialism	• Effective oral and written communication • Accessing analyzing information • Curiosity and imagination

21ST CENTURY SOFT SKILLS LinkedIn (2024)	
• Emotional intelligence • Problem-solving • Flexibility • Decision-making • Teamwork	• Creativity • Critical thinking • Collaboration • Adaptability • Time management

CHAPTER 14

····························

STANDOUT SCHOOL LEADERSHIP

The Hope of Schooling

*I*n this chapter I discuss the five qualities—vision, ideas, agenda leadership, enactment—that SSLs acquire over time that sets them apart from their AGJ colleagues. All school administrators possess the managerial and leadership tools to acquire these qualities and become SSLs. The remaining quality that sets all the other qualities in motion is the courage to expose the cracks in the grammar of schooling and the readiness to enact the organizational structures and pedagogies that restore hope to mission-driven goals and values.

> *It is easy to fall into the habit of regarding the mechanics of school organization and administration as something comparatively external and indifferent to educational purposes and ideals. We forget that it is precisely such things as these that really control the whole system even on its distinctively educational side.*
>
> —Dewey (1901)

"THERE ARE MAYBE THREE OR FOUR WHO STAND OUT"

I introduced this book by relating a remark made by one of the sports commentators during a Super Bowl game. In talking with his colleague about the various coaching strategies used during the game, the commentator stated that all coaches in the NFL were good at the job. They could never have attained a head coaching job in the NFL without exceptional knowledge of all aspects of the game. He ended the conversation with the observation that there were, however, three or four coaches in the league who stood out from the rest of the pack. In his words, "These . . . coaches just think differently about how the game should be played."

Most administrators are good at their jobs. This book is for AGJs who want to stand out from the pack, to think differently about the school game and to become SSLs. The preceding chapters in this book have presented ideas, beliefs, practices, and vocabularies that SSLs employ to close the gap between the institutional and global realities of schooling. This last chapter is devoted to describing the five qualities (see Figure 14.1) that all SSLs acquire over time to provide their communities with strategies for playing the game.

FIGURE 14.1   STANDOUT SCHOOL LEADERSHIP

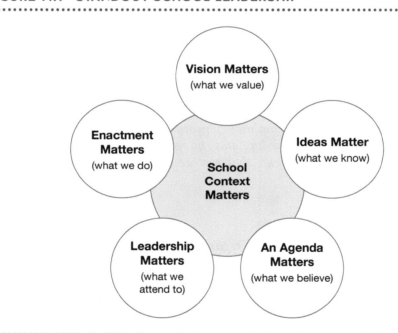

VISION MATTERS

All school districts have written into their policy manuals and marking materials a vision statement that lists the educational goals and practices they value. AGJs will reference one or more of these visionary pronouncements in public venues. When they return to their main offices, however, they frequently pay little or no attention to the goals and practices they are promoting on public stages. They accept school systems designed to accomplish institutional goals and practices. AGJs view the job as a matter of implementing policies, programs, and mandates passed down to them from governmental bodies and central offices. They do not view it as their job to question the beliefs, assumptions, or practices mandated by those governmental bodies. The function of implementation has no room for addressing the realities of the school they lead or for transforming mission-driven goals into operational practices.

SSLs refuse to accept the institutional realities of the schools they lead. Each day they ask themselves a series of questions about the classroom and the organizational realities occurring outside their offices:

> **SSLs refuse to accept the institutional realities of the schools they lead.**

- What reality of schooling am I working with in this school?
- Who is benefiting from this reality?
- Who is being hurt by this reality?
- Who is controlling this reality?
- What reality should we be pursuing?

If thoughtfully answered, each question exposes the gaps that exist between visionary goals and practices and the institutional realities that the school community experiences each day. SSLs view the job as a matter of designing and implementing organizational structures and teaching models that close the gap between institutional realities and educational ideals. The processes employed to close the gap between the *is* and the *ought* of schooling bring clarity to the educational ideals written into school mission statements.

IDEAS MATTER

School administrators will always find themselves lodged in the middle of four controlling influences in schooling: the interests of stakeholders, the goals and systems of institutions, the information that swirls in and out of schoolhouse doors, and the ideologies that describe the *why*, *what*, and *how* of schooling. AGJs often pay little attention to ideology. Most of their time is spent managing the interests, goals, and information that push and pull at their schools. They manage interests through political bartering. They manage goals by constructing efficient systems. They manage information by delegating it to a different party. They manage ideas by implementing programs and mandates. These managerial moves are lacking a framework of ideas in which interests, systems, and information work together to achieve a school-wide purpose.

SSLs view their primary role as making collective sense of the competing demands of special interest groups, the systems that govern the operations of the school, and the numerous ideas, research, opinions, and policies that flow around and into schools. To do this, SSLs must have a well-thought-out explanatory framework. This gives structure to how the aims, goals, and functions of a school will work together to provide a coherent understanding of how young people will be educated.

AN AGENDA MATTERS

No school community is a blank slate. All are populated with various constituencies that are more than willing to fill a school's agenda with their own interests, information, goals, and ideologies. AGJs spend their days managing this established agenda, and to it they add mission statements, TQM, strategic plans, data management systems, mandated programs, and the technique of the day. The benefit of a school's established agenda is that it offers something for everyone. The flaw is that the school lacks a clear purpose. Schools without a clear purpose or a coherent approach to teaching and learning will flounder from one program to another, from one crisis to another, from one year to another.

SSLs pursue a different approach to managing a school's agenda: They create their own. The foundation of that agenda is an interpretative framework composed of an instructional worldview, a narrative explaining that worldview, and strategies to use to implement the framework. An SSL's agenda seeks to weave the theories, concepts, ideas, and practices of teaching and learning into the everyday routines and understandings of the community they lead. On a daily basis, school administrators find themselves at a crossroads between established community/institutional agendas and mission-driven agendas. Frequently AGJs overlook the crossroads and focus solely on the established institutional highway. SSLs enter their schools with an agenda that navigates their community to the mission-driven exit off that highway.

LEADERSHIP MATTERS

AGJs and SSLs have fundamentally different perspectives about their roles in main offices. AGJs enter their offices every day focused on the *means* of schooling—planning, directing, and monitoring what is already in place—all of which are important, but not sufficient to stand out. SSLs focus on the *ends* of schooling—goals, values, and dispositions. AGJs lead with the *what* and *how*—good grades, accumulation of credits, diplomas, and admission to colleges. SSLs lead with the *why*—meaning, mastery, and inspiration.

The different orientations of AGJs and SSLs are on display every day. The calendar of one is populated with managerial activities, such as budget preparation, construction projects, technology installations, food service bids, and booster meetings. The calendar of the other is populated with instructional activities, such as teacher observations, postconferences, curriculum reviews, data analysis, and technology plans.

Both orientations adhere to the three principles of good leadership: clarity (the *why*), discipline (the *how*), and consistency (the *what*). AGJs and SSLs are both disciplined and consistent in carrying out their daily administrative functions. Where they depart from each other is their clarity over *which* functions should be carried out and how those functions should be performed.

Clarity makes known to the school community what school leaders care about, which defines the distinction between leadership and leading. Leadership—what AGJs model—is simply based on where you are positioned on organizational charts. Leading—what SSLs model—means that others are willing to follow you. SSLs, in what they attend to, in what they say, in what they ignore, and in what they champion, are clear that the *why* of schooling will drive the *what* and *how* of their schools.

> *AGJs and SSLs are both disciplined and consistent in carrying out their daily administrative functions. Where they depart from each other is their clarity over* which functions should be carried out and how those functions should be performed.

Teachers did not enter the profession of teaching to perform the routines of the *what* and *how* of schooling. Teachers entered the profession of teaching to participate with their colleagues in an undertaking that serves larger purposes than merely following routines.

ENACTMENT MATTERS

All the qualities of SSLs culminate in how school administrators think about and execute the tasks and functions of the job. AGJs view the execution function of the job as a matter of following rules, procedures, and programs—they paint by numbers. If a directive, mandate, or program does not fit into a school's organizational routines or classroom practices, an AGJ modifies it to fit established organizational and instructional practices.

SSLs view the execution function of the job as an opportunity to author a new reality of schooling by connecting the *why* of schooling to the *what* and *how* of a directive, mandate, or program. If a directive, mandate, or program does not fully serve a school's established *why*, SSLs either ignore the policy or redefine it to connect it with the *why*. Figure 14.2 summarizes the *why*, *what*, and *how* assumptions that govern the implementation process for AGJs (painting by numbers) and SSLs (connecting the dots).

The fundamental difference between these processes centers on the act of implementation. AGJs *implement* by mirroring the specifications of policies, mandates, or programs. SSLs see the *enactment* of a policy, mandate, or program as an opportunity to reauthor that policy, mandate, or program so it connects to an established *why* of schooling and also offers the possibility of generating a new reality of schooling. The distinction between the implementation and enactment processes symbolizes the essential qualities of an SSL: the willingness, the courage, and the skills to connect the established *how*s and *what*s of schooling to the mission-driven *why* of the school they lead.

FIGURE 14.2 PAINTING BY NUMBERS VERSUS CONNECTING THE DOTS

PAINTING BY NUMBERS (Implementation)	CONNECTING THE DOTS (Enactment)
• How	• Why
• Ends are predictable.	• Ends are uncertain.
• Means are prescribed by ends.	• Means are interpreted by ends.
• Knowledge is stable.	• Knowledge is generative.
• Teaching is learning techniques.	• Teaching is reflection on practice.
• Add-on programs/techniques are used.	• Assimilated programs/techniques are used.

STANDOUT SCHOOL LEADERSHIP
The Hope of Schooling

I have asked several colleagues of mine—all of whom are AGJs—to read chapters in this book. Their responses have all been some variation of, "Yes, Al, the profile of beliefs and behaviors of SSLs you describe would set those administrators apart from what we do in the trenches." However, they went on to lament that the strategies, tools, and practices described in these chapters are not sufficient to climb out of deep institutional trenches.

But in the course of these conversations, every colleague I spoke with was able to share at least one occasion when they employed their managerial and leadership skills to make their schools more interesting and more personalized. They *do* have the tools to climb out of the trenches, but it takes continual analysis and reframing to change existing habits of thoughts to employ those tools. Listening to the examples of how they made their schools more mission driven, I realized that in distinguishing between being good at your job and standing out beyond that, I may have inadvertently created a false dichotomy between being a good manager and being a good leader. The SSLs that I have described in this book possess both the managerial qualities to *do things well* and the leadership qualities to *do the right things*. The quality that sets an SSL apart from their colleagues is the courage to expose the cracks in the grammar of schooling and the readiness to enact organizational structures and pedagogies that restore hope to mission-driven goals and values.

> *They do have the tools to climb out of the trenches, but it takes continual analysis and reframing to change existing habits of thoughts to employ those tools.*

REFERENCES

Astor, R. A., Meyer, H. A., & Behre, W. J. (1999). Unowned places and times: Maps and interviews about violence in high schools. *American Educational Research Journal, 36,* 3–42.

Cremin, L. A. (1961). *The transformation of the school: Progressivism in American education, 1876–1957.* Knopf.

Cuban, L. (1984). *How teachers taught constancy and change in American classrooms: 1890–1980.* Research on teaching monograph series. Longman.

Dewar, C., Keller, S., & Malhotra, V. (2022). *CEO excellence: The six mindsets that distinguish the best leaders from the rest.* Scribner.

Dewey, J. (1901). The situation as regards the course of study. *Journal of the Proceedings and Addresses of the Fortieth Annual Meeting of the National Education Association,* 337–338.

Goodlad, J. I. (1984). *A place called school.* Association for Supervision and Curriculum Development.

Jackson, P. W. (1968). *Life in classrooms: Reissued with a new introduction.* Teachers College Press.

LinkedIn. (2024). *Profile surveys.* https://www.linkedin.com/pulse/essential-soft-hard-skills-job-seekers-21st-century-emran-hosen-vjw2c/

Trilling, B., & Fadel, C. (2009). *21st century skills: Learning for life in our times* (1st ed.). Jossey-Bass.

Tyack, D. B., & Tobin, W. (1994). The "grammar" of schooling: Why has it been so hard to change? *American Educational Research Journal, 31*(3), 453.

Wagner, T. (2008). *The global achievement gap: Why even our best schools don't teach the new survival skills our children need—and what we can do about it.* Basic Books.

INDEX

Solutions
YOU WANT

Experts
YOU TRUST

Results
YOU NEED

INSTITUTES

Corwin Institutes provide regional and virtual events where educators collaborate with peers and learn from industry experts. Prepare to be recharged and motivated!

corwin.com/institutes

ON-SITE PROFESSIONAL LEARNING

Corwin on-site PD is delivered through high-energy keynotes, practical workshops, and custom coaching services designed to support knowledge development and implementation.

www.corwin.com/pd

VIRTUAL PROFESSIONAL LEARNING

Our virtual PD combines live expert facilitation with the flexibility of anytime, anywhere professional learning. See the power of intentionally designed virtual PD.

www.corwin.com/virtualworkshops

CORWIN ONLINE

Online learning designed to engage, inform, challenge, and inspire. Our courses offer practical, classroom-focused instruction that will meet your continuing education needs and enhance your practice.

www.corwinonline.com

PLSN209A8

Visit **www.corwin.com**

A Sage Company

Helping educators make the greatest impact

CORWIN HAS ONE MISSION: to enhance education through intentional professional learning.

We build long-term relationships with our authors, educators, clients, and associations who partner with us to develop and continuously improve the best evidence-based practices that establish and support lifelong learning.